Red, White, and Sometimes Blue

CLASSICS from
McCall's QUILTING

Martingale®
& COMPANY

Red, White, and Sometimes Blue: Classics from *McCall's Quilting*

© 2011 by *McCall's Quilting*

That Patchwork Place® is an imprint of
Martingale & Company®.

Martingale & Company
19021 120th Ave. NE, Ste. 102
Bothell, WA 98011-9511 USA
www.martingale-pub.com

Mission Statement

Dedicated to providing quality products and service
to inspire creativity.

Credits

President & CEO: Tom Wierzbicki
Editor in Chief: Mary V. Green
Managing Editor: Tina Cook
Developmental Editor: Karen Costello Soltys
Design Director: Stan Green
Technical Editor: Robin Strobel
Copy Editor: Sheila Chapman Ryan
Production Manager: Regina Girard
Illustrator: Laurel Strand
Cover & Text Designer: Stan Green
Photographer: Mellisa Mahoney

McCall's Quilting, ISSN 1072-8395, is published bimonthly by
Creative Crafts Group, LLC, 741 Corporate Circle, Suite A, Golden,
CO, 80401, www.mccallsquilting.com.

Printed in China
16 15 14 13 12 11   8 7 6 5 4 3 2 1

**Library of Congress Cataloging-in-Publication Data is available
upon request.**

ISBN: 978-1-60468-051-5

Contents

Introduction

What images come to mind when you think of the colors red, white, and blue? Do you envision frilly Valentines, willowware and delft plates, and sparkling icicles? How about flags waving in the breeze or summer berry parfaits? Whether used in red-and-white or blue-and-white combinations or as a spirit-raising trio, these colors and the images they evoke are wonderful inspirations for classic quilts.

We've gathered a stunning group of red-and-white, blue-and-white, and red-white-and-blue quilts for this book. While many of the patterns would also lend themselves well to other color schemes, we hope you'll enjoy dipping into your red, white, and blue stash fabrics to stitch your own versions of these designer originals. Whether you're quilting to make a gift, to show patriotic pride, or to complement your home's interior; whether you're a new quilter or a seasoned hand; whether appliqué is your first love, or if you prefer patterns for pieced quilts, there are projects here to make the most of your precious sewing time.

There's a special energy created by one or two bold colors plus white. The combination is clean and direct, with a fabulous graphic punch. But there's also something especially comforting about these simple color schemes. They produce quilts with an heirloom look, as if Grandmother had stored them away for all her descendants to enjoy. These colors aren't subject to the fashion whims of the moment, so the quilts made with them are truly timeless. Be sure to apply labels to any quilts you make using the patterns in this book. Your creations are likely to be treasured by family and friends for many, many years to come.

Happy red, white, and blue quilting!

From the editors of
McCall's QUILTING

Red-and-White Quilts

WHETHER IT FEATURES ONE RED PRINT OR TWENTY, OR IF THE BACKGROUND IS PURE WHITE, OFF-WHITE, OR BEIGE, A RED-AND-WHITE QUILT COMMANDS ATTENTION. CHOOSE A BOLDLY GRAPHIC TWO-FABRIC QUILT OR DIP INTO YOUR SCRAPS FOR A RICHLY-HUED, ROMANTIC CHARMER. EITHER WAY, YOU'LL LOVE THE RESULTS.

Garnet Glaze

SPECIAL OCCASIONS ARE
THE PERFECT TIME TO GIVE
A QUILTED GIFT. THIS FUTURE
HEIRLOOM WAS MADE FOR
VICKI'S DAUGHTER AND
SON-IN-LAW AS A GIFT FOR
THEIR WEDDING.

Designed by Vicki Hoskins;
machine quilted by Jane Ann Houser

Finished quilt size: 73¾" x 93½"
Number and size of finished blocks: 18 Album blocks,
9⅞" x 9⅞"; 17 Connector blocks, 9⅞" x 9⅞"

Planning

What a gorgeous two-color quilt! The variety of red prints makes it sparkle. When selecting red fabrics, be sure to include lights, mediums, and darks, as well as a mix of prints and textures.

Notice the way the blocks are linked from corner to corner. To create this effect, Vicki very carefully planned the placement of the red fabrics in the block corners. Our instructions will guide you to do likewise (see "Connecting the Blocks," page 10).

Feel free to incorporate some of the appliqué fabrics in the blocks, as Vicki did. The yardages for the flower and leaf fabrics are sufficient for this purpose.

See page 11 for the appliqué patterns. The appliqué patterns are printed without seam allowances. The shapes are nearly symmetrical and do not need to be reversed for fusible appliqué.

Fabric Requirements

Dark red print (blocks, vines, flower centers, berry tops), 1¼ yards

Assorted red prints (blocks), 2 to 3 yards total*

White-on-white print (background), 4 yards

Red-and-cream print and cream-and-red print (flowers), ¼ yard each

Dark red swirl print (corner flowers), 9" x 9" piece

Red-and-white checked fabric (corner flower centers), 5" x 5" piece

Dark rust print (leaves), ¼ yard

Rose print (leaves), ¼ yard

Red-and-white dot print (strawberries), 6" x 10" piece

Red large-scale print (border, binding), 2½ yards

Backing (piece lengthwise), 5¾ yards

Batting, queen-size

⅜" bias bar (optional)

*See "Planning" at left.

Cutting Instructions

Dark red print:
    *4 bias strips, 1¼" x 80"
    90 squares, 2¼" x 2¼"
    20 using template B
    8 using template E

Assorted red prints:
    18 matching sets of 4 light squares, 2¼" x 2¼"
    36 matching sets of 4 medium squares, 2¼" x 2¼"
    18 matching sets of 8 medium/dark squares, 2¼" x 2¼"
    36 matching sets of:
        1 square, 2⅛" x 2⅛"; cut in half diagonally to make 2 half-square triangles (72 total)
        2 squares, 1¾" x 1¾" (72 total; 4 will be left over)

*Cut first.

White-on-white print:

*2 strips, 6½" x 74", cut on the lengthwise grain

*2 strips, 6½" x 66", cut on the lengthwise grain

*17 squares, 10⅜" x 10⅜"

54 squares, 3¾" x 3¾"; cut into quarters diagonally to make 216 quarter-square triangles

Red-and-cream print:

12 using template A

Cream-and-red print:

8 using template A

Dark red swirl print:

4 using template A

Red-and-white checked fabric:

4 using template B

Dark rust print:

50 using template C

Rose print:

46 using template C

Red-and-white dot print:

8 using template D

Red large-scale print:

2 strips, 6½" x 86", cut on the lengthwise grain

2 strips, 6½" x 78", cut on the lengthwise grain

4 strips, 2½" x 86", cut on the lengthwise grain (binding)

Cut first.

Piecing the Blocks

1. Piece the block center using sets of four assorted light red and four assorted medium red 2¼" squares and a dark red print 2¼" square.

2. Make four matching strips using a set of eight assorted medium/dark 2¼" squares and four dark red print 2¼" squares. Sew strips to opposite sides of the block center. Add white 3¾" quarter-square triangles to both ends of the remaining strips and sew to the top and bottom of the block center.

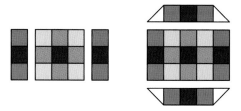

3. Using matching sets of four medium red 2¼" squares and eight white 3¾" quarter-square triangles, make pieced units for the block corners as shown; add to the block. Make a total of 18 cornerless Album blocks. Do not add the corners (assorted red 2⅛" half-square triangles) until the entire block arrangement is planned in the next step.

Make 18.

4. Refer to "Connecting the Blocks" to lay out the blocks, 10⅜" white squares, and matching sets of red triangles and 1¾" squares. Following a planned fabric arrangement, sew the triangles to the corners to complete an Album block. Return the block to its designated position on the design wall to confirm proper corner-fabric placement. Make 18 total Album blocks.

Album block.
Make 18.

5. To piece the Connector blocks, draw a diagonal line on the wrong side of each selected 1¾" red square with the marking tool of your choice. Refer to your fabric arrangement to place the red squares in planned locations on the corners of a white 10⅜" square, right sides together and aligning raw edges. Stitch on the drawn lines; trim away and discard the excess fabric. Press open. Return to the design wall to confirm proper corner-fabric arrangement. Make 17 total Connector blocks.

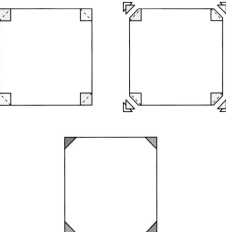

Connector block.
Make 17.

Use a design wall, bed, or floor to plan your block arrangement. Alternating cornerless Album blocks with white 10⅜" squares, lay out seven rows of five blocks or squares each.

Place a matching set of two half-square triangles and two squares at each intersection of four blocks. Pin the squares to the appropriate corners of the white 10⅜" squares. Pin the matching triangles to the appropriate corners of the adjacent cornerless Album blocks.

Once all the corner fabrics have been assigned to the four-block intersections, arrange the remaining red triangles and squares along the quilt edges, matching adjacent corner fabrics.

When sewing the corner triangles to the Album blocks and when making the Connector blocks, work on one block at a time and return each to its designated position in the quilt layout once it's been stitched.

Quilt-Top Assembly

Referring to the quilt assembly diagram above right, sew seven rows of five blocks each. Sew the rows together. Stitch the white 6½" x 74" strips to the sides; trim even with the top and bottom. Stitch the remaining white strips to the top and bottom; trim even with the sides. Sew the red large-scale print 6½" x 86" strips to the sides; trim even. Sew the remaining red strips to the top and bottom; trim even.

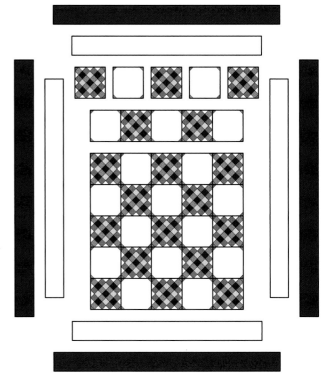

Quilt assembly

Appliquéing the Border

1. Fold a dark red print 1¼" x 80" bias strip in half, wrong sides together. Stitch ¼" from the raw edge. Trim the seam allowance to ⅛". Press the tube flat, centering the seam allowance on the back so the raw edge isn't visible from the front. Using a ⅜" bias bar makes pressing faster and easier. Make four.

2. Referring to the quilt photo (page 9) for vine placement, position the prepared vines and trim if needed. Using the appliqué method of your choice (see "Appliqué" on page 90), appliqué in place. Position and appliqué all the template pieces to complete the quilt top.

Quilting and Finishing

Layer, baste, and quilt (see "Finishing" on page 94). The quilt shown was machine quilted with monofilament on the white fabric and red thread on the red fabrics. A feathered wreath with a stippled center is stitched in each Connector block. Undulating feather motifs cover the red block fabrics. The remaining white areas are quilted with a close meander. A continuous undulating feather fills the outer border. The appliqués are quilted in the ditch. Bind the quilt with the red large-scale print 2½"-wide strips.

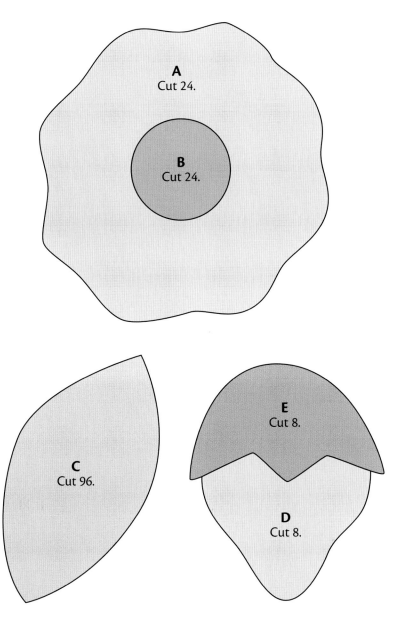

A
Cut 24.

B
Cut 24.

C
Cut 96.

E
Cut 8.

D
Cut 8.

A GIFT FOR HER SON MATTHEW, AN ASPIRING WRITER, KELLY CORBRIDGE'S STUNNING QUILT DESIGN EVOKES THE TWISTS, TURNS, AND OCCASIONAL DEAD ENDS OF AN AUTHOR'S WORK. GORGEOUS MACHINE QUILTING COMPLETES THIS TIMELESS HEIRLOOM LOOK.

Designed by Kelly Corbridge; machine quilted by Julie Lambert

Finished quilt size: 76½" x 94½"

Number and size of finished blocks: 12 Checkerboard Path blocks, 15" x 15"

Planning

Kelly was inspired by a vintage scrap quilt in the book *American Quilts and How to Make Them* (Charles Scribner's Sons, 1975), written by Carter Houck and Myron Miller. The original quilt featured 1½" finished squares, which yielded 22½" finished blocks.

Fabric Requirements

Red tone-on-tone print (blocks, sashing), 2⅛ yards

White solid (blocks, sashing, border, binding), 7 yards

Backing (piece widthwise), 7⅛ yards

Batting, queen-size

Cutting Instructions

Red tone-on-tone print:
>   46 strips, 1½" x 42"

White solid:
>   *4 strips, 10" x 80", cut on the lengthwise grain
>   42 strips, 1½" x 42"
>   4 strips, 2½" x 42"
>   48 strips, 3½" x 9½"
>   62 squares, 3½" x 3½"
>   9 strips, 2½" x 42" (binding)

Cut first.

Piecing the Blocks

1. Sew two red and one white 1½" strips together. Make 14 strip sets. Press the seam allowances as shown. Cut 363 segments, 1½" wide. Repeat using two white and one red 1½" strips. Make 14 strip sets. Press and cut 348 segments, 1½" wide.

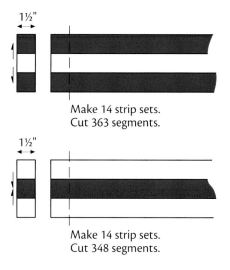

1½"

Make 14 strip sets.
Cut 363 segments.

1½"

Make 14 strip sets.
Cut 348 segments.

2. Sew together a white 2½" strip and a red 1½" strip. Make four. Press and cut 96 segments, 1½" wide.

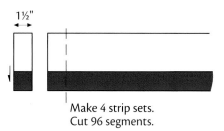

1½"

Make 4 strip sets.
Cut 96 segments.

3. Sew the segments from steps 1 and 2 together in the quantities and combinations shown to make pieced squares.

Make 94. Make 79. Make 96.

4. Arrange and sew three rows using three pieced squares each as shown, watching the orientation. Sew the rows together to make a block center.

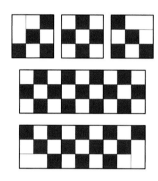

5. Stitch white 9½" strips to opposite sides of the block center. Sew pieced squares to both ends of two 9½" white strips as shown. Stitch these strips to the top and bottom of the block center to make a Checkerboard Path block. Make 12.

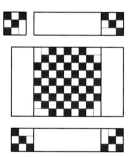 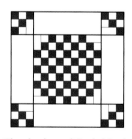

Checkerboard Path block.
Make 12.

Piecing the Sashing

Sew three pieced squares and two white 3½" squares together to make a sashing strip. Make 31.

Make 31.

Quilt-Top Assembly

Refer to the quilt assembly diagram for the following steps.

1. Sew five sashing rows using four pieced squares and three sashing strips for each.

2. Stitch four block rows using four sashing strips and three blocks each.

3. Sew the rows together, alternating the sashing and block rows.

4. Stitch white 80" strips to the sides of the quilt top; trim them even with the top and bottom. Sew the remaining 80" white strips to the top and bottom of the quilt top; trim them even with the sides.

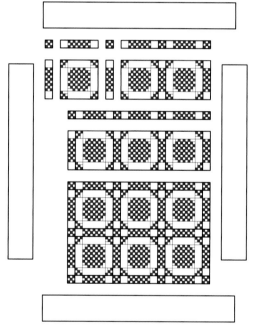

Quilt assembly

Quilting and Finishing

Layer, baste, and quilt (see "Finishing" on page 94). Julie's elaborate machine quilting gives an antique look. Feathered wreaths are quilted around the center checkerboard areas of each block. The small red and white squares are each stitched with an X, forming diagonal lines across the piecing. Small floral motifs are centered in the white 3½" squares. The border features a feathered vine. The remainder of the border is filled with straight lines stitched perpendicular to the binding. Bind with the white solid strips.

WHAT'S RED, WHITE, AND SPECIAL ALL OVER? THIS PRETTY STAR-STUDDED THROW, MADE WITH LOVE . . . BY YOU! DOROTHY'S QUILT SHOWCASES BEAUTIFUL RED-AND-WHITE PRINTS THAT COMBINE TO MAKE A CHARMING WALL HANGING OR A SNUGGLY THROW FOR YOUR FAVORITE VALENTINE.

Finished quilt size: 67½" x 67½"

Number and size of finished blocks: 1 Small Star block, 6" x 6"; 1 Large Star block, 18" x 18"; 8 Medium Star blocks, 9" x 9"; 4 Nine Patch blocks, 9" x 9"; 4 Box blocks, 9" x 9"

Fabric Requirements

White sprig print (blocks, borders), 1¼ yards

Red small floral print (blocks, borders), 1⅛ yards

White vine print (blocks), ⅞ yard

White large floral print (blocks, borders), 1¼ yards

Red large floral print (blocks, borders, binding), 2⅜ yards

White small floral print (blocks), ⅜ yard

Backing, 4⅜ yards

Batting, full-size

Designed by Dorothy Ann Weld; machine quilted by Pat Kilmark

Cutting Instructions

White sprig print:
- *6 strips, 2½" x 42"
- *2 strips, 2¾" x 42"; cut each strip into 1 piece, 23" long, and 1 piece, 18½" long
- *1 square, 7¼" x 7¼"
- 1 square, 3¼" x 3¼"
- 8 squares, 4¼" x 4¼"
- 4 rectangles, 2" x 3½"
- 4 rectangles, 2" x 6½"

Red small floral print:
- *6 strips, 1½" x 42"
- *2 strips, 2¾" x 27½"
- *2 strips, 2¾" x 23"
- *2 squares, 7¼" x 7¼"
- 2 squares, 3¼" x 3¼"
- 16 squares, 4¼" x 4¼"

White vine print:
- *1 square, 7¼" x 7¼"
- *4 squares, 6½" x 6½"
- 1 square, 3¼" x 3¼"
- 8 squares, 4¼" x 4¼"
- 4 squares, 2½" x 2½"
- 32 squares, 3½" x 3½"

White large floral print:
- *8 strips, 4½" x 42"
- *8 squares, 3½" x 3½"
- 1 square, 2½" x 2½"

Red large floral print:
- *8 strips, 2½" x 42" (binding)
- *14 strips, 2½" x 42"
- 24 squares, 3½" x 3½"
- 4 rectangles, 2" x 6½"
- 8 rectangles, 2" x 8"
- 4 rectangles, 2" x 9½"

White small floral print:
- 16 squares, 3½" x 3½"
- 8 rectangles, 2" x 5"

*Cut first.

Piecing the Blocks

1. Draw diagonal lines from corner to corner, one in each direction, on the wrong side of the white sprig print 3¼" square. Place the marked square on a red small floral 3¼" square, right sides together. Sew a ¼" seam on each side of one line. Cut the squares apart, cutting on the unsewn line first, and then cut the pieces apart on the remaining drawn line to yield four sets of quarter-square-triangle pairs. Press open. Repeat with the white vine print and remaining red small floral 3¼" squares to make four more sets of pieced triangles.

Make 4.   Make 4.

2. In the same manner, make pieced triangles with the white sprig and white vine prints in the sizes and quantities shown.

7¼"

Make 4.   Make 4.

4¼"

Make 32.   Make 32.

3. Sew a red 3¼" floral/white sprig pieced triangle to a red small floral/vine print pieced triangle to make a pieced square. Make four. Repeat in the sizes and quantities shown.

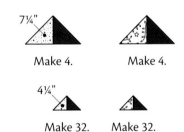

Vine print

Sprig print

Make 4 from 3¼" triangles.   Make 4 from 7¼" triangles.   Make 32 from 4¼" triangles.

4. Stitch together four vine print 2½" squares, four small pieced squares, and a white large floral 2½" square to make one Small Star block. Orient the white sprig print in the pieced squares toward the center.

Small Star block.
Make 1.

5. In the same manner, join four vine print 6½" squares, four large pieced squares, and the Small Star block to make a Large Star block.

Large Star block.
Make 1.

6. Stitch together four vine print 3½" squares, four medium pieced squares, and one white large floral 3½" square to make a Medium Star block. Repeat to make a total of eight blocks.

Medium Star block.
Make 8.

7. Stitch together five red large floral and four white small floral 3½" squares to make a Nine Patch block. Repeat to make a total of four blocks.

Nine Patch block.
Make 4.

8. Sew red and white 2"-wide rectangles to a red large floral 3½" square as shown to make four Box blocks.

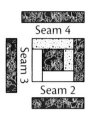

Box block.
Make 4.

Quilt-Top Assembly

1. Stitch the white sprig 18½" strips to the sides of the Large Star block. Sew the white sprig 23" strips to the top and bottom. Stitch the red small floral 23" strips to the sides. Sew the red small floral 27½" strips to the top and bottom.

2. Sew a Nine Patch block between two Medium Star blocks. Repeat to make a total of four units. Sew two of these units to opposite sides of the quilt top. Stitch the Box blocks to both ends of the remaining block units. Stitch these units to the top and bottom of the quilt top.

3. Piece the border strips together end to end to make the following lengths:
   Four 1½" x 52" red small floral strips (border 1)
   Four 2½" x 56" white sprig strips (border 2)
   Four 2½" x 60" red large floral strips (border 3)
   Four 4½" x 68" white large floral strips (border 4)
   Four 2½" x 72" red large floral strips (border 5)

   Sew the 52" strips to opposite sides of the quilt top; trim even with the top and bottom. Stitch the remaining 52" strips to the top and bottom; trim even with the sides. In the same manner, add the remaining four borders in the given order.

Quilting and Finishing

Layer, baste, and quilt (see "Finishing" on page 94). Pat machine quilted a feather design in the Large Star block, a meander in the inner borders, a heart-shaped vine design in the outer borders, and a different design in each 9" block. Bind with the 2½"-wide red large floral strips.

Sweetheart Stars

ROMANTIC, YES, BUT MEN WILL LIKE IT TOO! SAY "I LOVE YOU" WITH THIS JUST-SWEET-ENOUGH TREAT.

Designed by Vicki Hoskins;
machine quilted by Jane Ann Houser

Cutting Instructions

Medium pink print:
> *4 strips, 1" x 44", cut on the lengthwise grain
> 36 squares, 2⅜" x 2⅜"; cut in half diagonally to make 72 half-square triangles
> 18 squares, 2⅜" x 2⅜"
> 8 using template B

Burgundy print:
> 36 each using template A and A reversed
> 8 using template D

Cherry red print:
> 9 squares, 4¼" x 4¼"; cut into quarters diagonally to make 36 quarter-square triangles

Black solid:
> *4 strips, ¾" x 45", cut on the lengthwise grain
> *6 strips, 2½" x 42", cut on the lengthwise grain (binding)
> 18 squares, 2⅜" x 2⅜"
> 8 bias-cut strips, 1¼" x 16½"
> 36 using template B

Red paisley:
> *4 strips, 6½" x 57", cut on the lengthwise grain
> 72 squares, 2" x 2"
> 9 squares, 3½" x 3½"
> 16 using template B

White solid:
> *4 strips, 5½" x 43", cut on the lengthwise grain
> 36 rectangles, 2" x 3½"

Red-and-cream print:
> 36 squares, 2" x 2"
> 8 using template C

Cut first.

Finished quilt size: 51" x 51"

Number and size of finished blocks: 9 Lattice Star blocks, 9" x 9"

Planning

The strips for vines are cut on the bias. Appliqué patterns B, C, and D (page 25) are printed without seam allowances. Piecing pattern A (page 25) already contains a seam allowance. (See "Making Templates" on page 89.) When cutting piece A, place two pieces of fabric right sides together and cut through both layers. You'll get one regular piece and one piece reversed. You can also cut one layer of fabric and flip the template so that the right side is down to reverse the pattern.

Fabric Requirements

Medium pink print (blocks, buds, narrow border), 1⅜ yards

Burgundy print (blocks, flower centers), ½ yard

Cherry red print (blocks), ¼ yard

Black solid (blocks, vines, leaves, narrow border, binding), 1⅜ yards

Red paisley (blocks, buds, outer border), 1¾ yards

White solid (blocks, inner border), ⅜ yard

Red-and-cream print (blocks, flowers), ⅜ yard

Backing, 3½ yards

Batting, twin-size

⅜" bias bar (optional)

Piecing the Blocks

1. Sew two medium pink print 2⅜" half-square triangles, a piece A and a piece A reversed, and a cherry red print 4¼" quarter-square triangle together to make a pieced rectangle. Make 36.

Make 36.

2. On the wrong side of a medium pink 2⅜" square, draw a diagonal line with the marking tool of your choice. Place the pink square on a black 2⅜" square, right sides together. Sew a ¼" seam on each side of the marked line; cut apart on the marked line. Press open to make pieced squares. Make 36.

Make 36.

3. Draw a diagonal line on the wrong side of a red paisley 2" square. Place the red square on a white 2" x 3½" rectangle, right sides together and aligning raw edges. Stitch on the drawn line; trim away and discard the excess fabric. Press open. Repeat on the opposite end of the white rectangle to make a flying-geese unit. Make 36.

Make 36.

4. Arrange and sew three rows using four pieced squares, four flying-geese units, and a red paisley 3½" square. Sew the rows together to make a block center. Make nine.

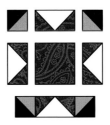

Make 9.

5. Arrange and sew three rows using four red-and-cream 2" squares, four pieced rectangles, and a block center. Sew the rows together to complete a Lattice Star block. Repeat to make nine blocks.

Lattice Star block.
Make 9.

Quilt-Top Assembly and Appliqué

Refer to the quilt assembly diagram on page 24 for the following steps.

1. Stitch three rows of three blocks each. Sew the rows together.

2. Fold a white 5½" x 43" strip in half; press the fold to mark the center. In the same manner, fold and press a medium pink 1" x 44" strip, a black ¾" x 45" strip, and a red paisley 6½" x 57" strip. Open the folds and sew the strips together, matching the center fold lines. Repeat to make four border strips.

Align creases.

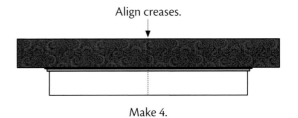

Make 4.

3. Finger-press the quilt top in half lengthwise and crosswise; use the folds as placement lines. Pin the prepared border strips to the sides of the quilt, matching the center fold lines. Starting and stopping ¼" from the quilt corners, sew the pieced borders to all four sides of the quilt. Referring to "Borders" (page 93), miter the corners.

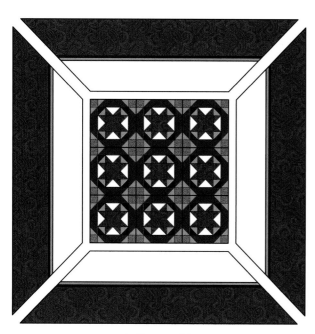

Quilt assembly

4. To make the vine, fold a black bias-cut 1¼" x 16½" strip in half, wrong sides together. Stitch ¼" from the raw edge. Trim the seam allowance to ⅛". Press the tube flat, centering the seam allowance on the back so the raw edge isn't visible from the front. Using a ⅜" bias bar makes pressing faster and easier. Trim the ends so the strip measures 15". Make eight strips.

5. Referring to the photo on page 22, position the vines on the white border. Using the appliqué method of your choice (see "Appliqué" on page 90), position pieces B, C, and D; appliqué in place.

Top/bottom border appliqué placement

Side border appliqué placement

Quilting and Finishing

Layer, baste , and quilt (see "Finishing" on page 94). Jane Ann machine quilted an overall feathered pattern in the quilt center and outer border. She outline stitched the appliqué and filled the white border with an echo-quilted floral pattern. Bind the quilt with the 2½"-wide black solid strips.

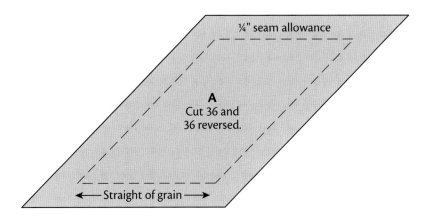

¼" seam allowance

A
Cut 36 and
36 reversed.

← Straight of grain →

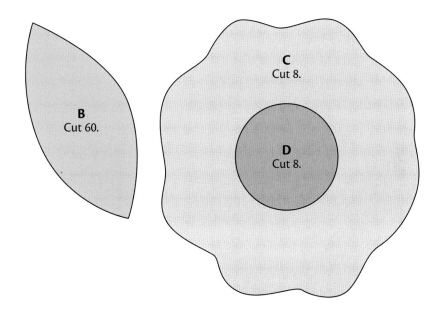

B
Cut 60.

C
Cut 8.

D
Cut 8.

Two Simple!

READY . . . SET . . . SEW!

FIND A BRIGHT OR DARK PRINT FABRIC THAT YOU LOVE, ADD A WHITE PRINT, AND YOU'VE GOT INSTANT DRAMA WITH JUST TWO FABRICS. BE SURE TO USE AN ACCURATE ¼" SEAM ALLOWANCE DURING CONSTRUCTION AND YOU CAN MAKE THIS STRIKING QUILT IN A WEEKEND.

Finished quilt size: 82½" x 90½"

Number and size of finished blocks: 110 Nine Patch Variation blocks, 8" x 8"

Fabric Requirements

White-on-white print (piecing), 4½ yards

Red-on-red swirl print (piecing, binding), 5¼ yards

Backing (piece widthwise), 7¾ yards

Batting, queen-size

Designed by Janice Davis;
machine quilted by Lisa Marshall of Quilter's Treats, Inc.

Cutting Instructions

White-on-white print:

12 strips, 1½" x 42"

6 strips, 6½" x 42"

10 strips, 6½" x 42"; cut into 55 squares, 6½" x 6½"

4 strips, 6½" x 42"; cut into 110 rectangles, 1½" x 6½"

2 squares, 1½" x 1½"

Red-on-red swirl print:

12 strips, 1½" x 42"

6 strips, 6½" x 42"

10 strips, 6½" x 42"; cut into 55 squares, 6½" x 6½"

4 strips, 6½" x 42"; cut into 110 rectangles, 1½" x 6½"

2 squares, 1½" x 1½"

9 strips, 2½" x 42" (binding)

Piecing the Blocks

1. Sew white 1½" strips to the long sides of a red 6½" strip to make a strip set. Repeat to make six. Press the seam allowances as shown. Cut the strip sets into a total of 131 segments, 1½" wide. In the same manner, sew red 1½" strips to the long sides of a white 6½" strip. Repeat to make six. Press the seam allowances as shown and cut into 131 segments, 1½" wide.

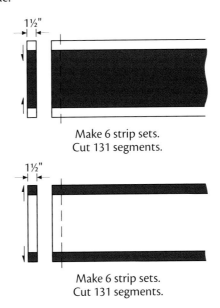

Make 6 strip sets.
Cut 131 segments.

Make 6 strip sets.
Cut 131 segments.

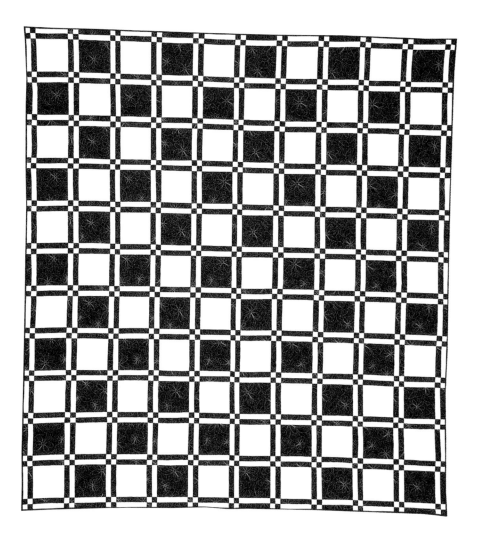

2. Sew red 1½" x 6½" rectangles to the top and bottom of the white 6½" squares. Sew units from step 1 to the sides as shown to make 55 Nine Patch Variation blocks. In the same manner, sew white 1½" x 6½" rectangles to the red 6½" squares. Add units from step 1 to make 55 Nine Patch Variation blocks in the opposite color arrangement.

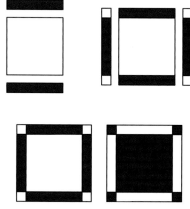

Make 55.   Make 55.

Quilt-Top Assembly

Refer to the quilt assembly diagram below for the following steps.

1. Sew 11 rows of 10 blocks each, alternating the color arrangements. Sew the rows together.

2. To make the left pieced border, stitch six white and five red segments from step 1 together end to end, alternating the colors. Sew to the left side of the quilt. To make the right pieced border, sew six red and five white segments together, alternating the colors. Sew this border to the right side of the quilt.

3. To make the top and bottom borders, stitch five red and five white segments together, alternating the colors. Sew a white and a red 1½" square to opposite ends of the border. Make two; sew them to the quilt top and bottom.

Quilting and Finishing

Layer, baste, and quilt (see "Finishing" on page 94). Lisa used white thread and machine quilted a continuous flower and leaf design across the quilt, adding pattern and dimension to the surface. Bind with the red 2½"-wide strips.

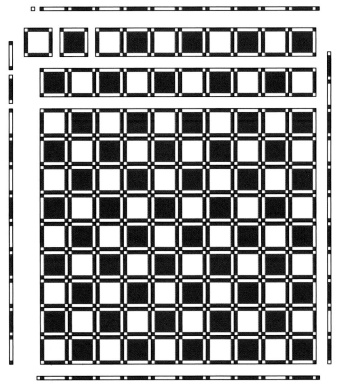

Quilt assembly

Heart's Desire

THIS CHARMING LITTLE QUILT FEATURES LOVELY QUILTING DONE IN RED THREAD, A BEAUTIFUL HAND-STITCHED FINISH TO THIS FAST-TO-PIECE PROJECT.

Finished quilt size: 25½" x 25½"

Number and size of finished blocks: 5 Woven Heart blocks, 6" x 6"

Planning

Each block is made using the patches cut from one tan print and one red print. For a more contemporary look, substitute assorted white prints for the tan patches in the blocks and a different white print for the cream mottled print used in the setting triangles and middle border.

Fabric Requirements

5 assorted tan prints (blocks), ⅛ yard each

5 assorted red prints (blocks), ⅛ yard each

Cream mottled print (setting triangles, middle border), ¾ yard

Red swirl print (inner and outer borders, binding), ⅝ yard

Backing, 1 yard

Batting, 32" x 32" square

Cutting Instructions

5 assorted tan prints—cut from each:

*1 square, 2¾" x 2¾"

1 rectangle, 1" x 1¼"

1 rectangle, 1" x 1¾"

1 strip, 1" x 2¼"

1 strip, 1" x 2¾"

1 strip, 1" x 3¼"

1 strip, 1" x 3¾"

4 squares, 1½" x 1½"

5 assorted red prints—cut from each:

*2 rectangles, 2¾" x 4¼"

1 square, 1¼" x 1¼"

1 rectangle, 1" x 1¾"

1 strip, 1" x 2¼"

1 strip, 1" x 2¾"

1 strip, 1" x 3¼"

1 strip, 1" x 3¾"

1 strip, 1" x 4¼"

Cream mottled print:

*4 strips, 3" x 26"

1 square, 11" x 11"; cut into quarters diagonally to make 4 quarter-square triangles

2 squares, 6" x 6"; cut in half diagonally to make 4 half-square triangles

Red swirl print:

4 strips, 1¼" x 20"

4 strips, 1¼" x 28"

3 strips, 2½" x 42" (binding)

*Cut first.

Piecing the Blocks

1. Sew a tan 1" x 1¼" rectangle to the bottom of a red 1¼" square. Sew a matching tan 1" x 1¾" rectangle to the left side. Stitch a matching red 1" x 1¾" rectangle to the bottom. Stitch a matching red 1" x 2¼" strip to the left side. Continue to add tan and red strips in the sizes shown to make a pieced square. Make five pieced squares total, using the same red and tan fabrics consistently throughout each block.

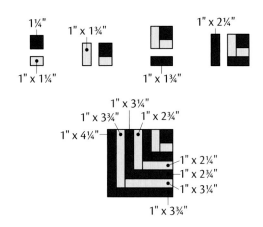

2. Draw a diagonal line on the wrong side of a matching tan 1½" square. Place the marked square on a matching red 2¾" x 4¼" rectangle, right sides together and aligning the raw edges. Stitch on the drawn line; trim away and discard the excess fabric. Repeat on the opposite corner to make a pieced rectangle. Make five sets of two matching units.

3. Sew two rows using two matching pieced rectangles, a 2¾" square, and a pieced square. Sew the rows together to make a Woven Heart block. Make five total.

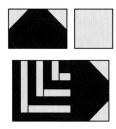 

Woven Heart block.
Make 5.

Quilt-Top Assembly

Refer to the quilt assembly diagram for the following steps. The setting triangles on all edges and corners are cut oversized to allow trimming the quilt edges even after assembly.

1. Sew three diagonal rows using the Woven Heart blocks and the 11" cream quarter-square triangles. Sew the rows together. Stitch the cream 6" half-square triangles to the quilt-top corners. Trim the edges even.

2. Stitch red 20" strips to opposite sides of the quilt top; trim even with the top and bottom. Stitch the remaining red 20" strips to the top and bottom of the quilt top; trim even with the sides. Sew the cream 26" strips to the quilt top in the same manner. Then add the red 28" strips.

Quilt assembly

Quilting and Finishing

Layer, baste, and quilt (see "Finishing" on page 94). Joyce hand quilted using red thread. She stitched in the ditch around all the red block patches and filled the setting triangles with feathered heart motifs. The cream border strips feature a rope design centered with a heart. Bind with the 2½" red swirl print strips.

Célébrer!

USING YOUR FAVORITE PRINTS IN THE LARGE SQUARES WILL MAKE THIS QUILT A CELEBRATION OF FABRIC. DON'T LET THE NUMBER OF TRIANGLES INTIMIDATE YOU! THE DESIGN IS FUN TO PUT TOGETHER, AND ATTRACTIVE WITH LIGHT AND DARK FABRICS IN ANY COLOR OF YOUR CHOICE.

Designed by Lissa Alexander; machine quilted by Matt Sparrow of ManQuilter.com

Fabric Requirements

Assorted red and dark pink prints (blocks), 15 fat quarters* total

Assorted cream, taupe, and light gray prints (blocks), 2 fat quarters* total

**Red-and-white striped fabric (blocks), 10" x 20" piece

**Taupe-red-and-white striped fabric (blocks), 10" x 20" piece

**Tan-and-cream striped fabric (blocks), 10" x 10" piece

**Taupe-and-cream large striped fabric (blocks), 10" x 10" piece

Light gray print (inner border), ⅝ yard

Cream-and-red small floral (middle border), ½ yard

Dark pink large floral (outer border), 2½ yards

Taupe-and-cream small striped fabric (bias-cut binding), 1 yard

Backing (piece lengthwise), 5½ yards

Batting, queen-size

*A fat quarter is an 18" x 20–22" cut of fabric.
**These are heavier woven striped fabrics.

Finished quilt size: 70½" x 94½"

Number and size of finished blocks: 15 A blocks, 8" x 8"; 12 B blocks, 8" x 8"; 27 C blocks, 8" x 8"

Planning

Rich in color and oh-so-appealing, this classic Ocean Waves quilt is made of just three simple blocks. When making her quilt, Lissa used both quilting fabrics and heavier woven striped fabrics, giving the quilt a tantalizing change of textures. She also substituted a few 2⅞" squares cut from the border and binding fabrics for those listed in the "Cutting Instructions" on the facing page. If you wish to do likewise, cut the border and binding strips first.

Cutting Instructions

Assorted red and dark pink prints—cut a total of:
270 squares, 2⅞" x 2⅞"
18 squares, 6³⁄₁₆" x 6³⁄₁₆"*
54 squares, 2⅞" x 2⅞"; cut in half diagonally to make 108 half-square triangles

Assorted cream, taupe, and light gray prints—cut a total of:
270 squares, 2⅞" x 2⅞"
3 squares, 6³⁄₁₆" x 6³⁄₁₆"*
54 squares, 2⅞" x 2⅞"; cut in half diagonally to make 108 half-square triangles

*6³⁄₁₆" is midway between 6⅛" and 6¼" on your ruler.

Red-and-white striped and taupe-red-and-white striped fabrics—cut from each:

2 squares, 6³⁄₁₆" x 6³⁄₁₆"*, cut on the bias grain (4 total)

Tan-and-cream striped and taupe-and-cream large striped fabrics—cut from each:

1 square, 6³⁄₁₆" x 6³⁄₁₆"*, cut on the bias grain (2 total)

Light gray print:

2 strips, 2½" x 76", pieced from 4 strips, 2½" x 42"

2 strips, 2½" x 56", pieced from 3 strips, 2½" x 42"

Cream-and-red small floral:

2 strips, 1½" x 80", pieced from 4 strips, 1½" x 42"

2 strips, 1½" x 60", pieced from 3 strips, 1½" x 42"

Dark pink large floral:

4 strips, 8½" x 82", cut on the lengthwise grain

Taupe-and-cream small striped fabric:

1 square, 32" x 32" (binding). Refer to "Cutting Continuous Bias Strips from a Square" (page 94) for 2½"-wide bias-cut binding.

*6³⁄₁₆" is midway between 6⅛" and 6¼" on your ruler.

Piecing the Blocks

Pay careful attention to the positioning and orientation of colors throughout.

1. Draw a diagonal line from corner to corner on the wrong side of an assorted light 2⅞" square. Place the marked square on an assorted red 2⅞" square, right sides together. Sew a ¼" seam on each side of the marked line; cut apart on the marked line. Press open to make two pieced squares. Make 540 total.

Make 540.

2. Stitch two rows of two pieced squares each, orienting light and dark fabrics as shown. Sew the rows together to make a pieced unit. Make 108 total.

Make 108.

3. Sew two rows of two units each, rotating the units as shown. Stitch the rows together to make an A block. Make 15 total.

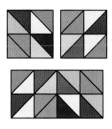

Block A.
Make 15.

4. In the same manner but reversing the positions of the colors, make 12 total B blocks.

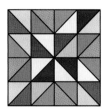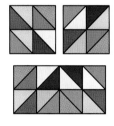

Block B.
Make 12.

5. Stitch together one pieced square from step 1 and two assorted light 2⅞" half-square triangles to make a pieced triangle. Make 54 total. In the same manner, stitch together one pieced square and two assorted red 2⅞" half-square triangles to make a pieced triangle. Make 54 total.

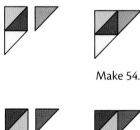

Make 54.

Make 54.

6. Stitch together one of the assorted 6³⁄₁₆" squares and two pieced triangles of each color arrangement to make a C block. Make 27 total.

Block C.
Make 27.

Quilt-Top Assembly

Refer to the quilt assembly diagram and the photo on the facing page for the following steps.

1. Sew nine rows of six blocks each, watching placement and orientation. Stitch the rows together.

2. Stitch the light gray print 76" strips to the sides; trim even with the top and bottom. Sew the light gray 56" strips to the top and bottom; trim even with the sides. Sew the cream-and-red 80" strips to the sides;

trim even. Stitch the cream-and-red 60" strips to the top and bottom; trim even. Sew two of the dark pink large floral strips to the sides; trim even. Sew the remaining dark pink large floral strips to the top and bottom; trim even.

Quilting and Finishing

Layer, baste, and quilt (see "Finishing" on page 94). Using variegated red thread, Matt machine quilted eight-pointed stars in the large squares and arcing lines connecting the corners of each triangle. The inner border features an arc-and-loop motif and the middle border has a connected triangle motif. The outer border is filled with large flowers. Bind with the 2½" bias-cut taupe-and-cream fabric.

Explore Your Options

Fabric reproductions from the '30s and '40s combine with squares cut from vintage embroidered tea towels in this sweet variation on Lissa's design.

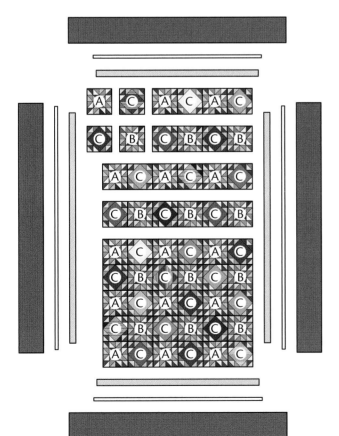

Quilt assembly

Blue-and-White Quilts

COOL AND CRISP, A BLUE-AND-WHITE COLOR SCHEME IS
AT ONCE CALMING AND REJUVENATING. IT'S BEEN SAID
THAT BLUE IS THE BEST COLOR FOR A BEDROOM BECAUSE
IT'S SO RESTFUL. NO WONDER BLUE-AND-WHITE QUILTS
HAVE BEEN POPULAR FOR NEARLY 200 YEARS!

Duty, Honor, Country

ONE IN A SERIES OF CIVIL WAR QUILTS, THIS ONE IS BASED ON THE TRADITIONAL OHIO STAR BLOCK. KELLY MADE THIS FOR HER SON NATE, A GRADUATE OF WEST POINT, WHERE "DUTY, HONOR, COUNTRY" IS A PROUD MOTTO.

Designed and quilted by Kelly Corbridge

Finished quilt size: 84½" x 99½"

Number and size of finished blocks: 20 Ohio Star Variation blocks, 10⅝" x 10⅝"

Planning

When working with lots of small pieces, an accurate ¼" seam allowance is critical. We suggest you double-check your piecing accuracy by making a test block. It should measure 11⅛" square, raw edge to raw edge.

Fabric Requirements

White solid (blocks, background, border, binding), 8¾ yards

Indigo small print (blocks, pieced border), 2⅛ yards

Backing (piece widthwise), 7⅞ yards

Batting, queen-size

Cutting Instructions

White solid:
- *4 strips, 9½" x 89", cut on the lengthwise grain
- *4 squares, 17" x 17"; cut into quarters diagonally to make 16 quarter-square triangles (2 left over)
- *12 squares, 11⅛" x 11⅛"
- *10 strips, 2½" x 42" (binding)
- 120 squares, 3⅜" x 3⅜"
- 180 squares, 2⅝" x 2⅝"
- 2 squares, 9" x 9"; cut in half diagonally to make 4 half-square triangles
- 45 squares, 4¼" x 4¼"; cut into quarters diagonally to make 180 quarter-square triangles
- 8 squares, 2⅜" x 2⅜"; cut in half diagonally to make 16 half-square triangles

Indigo small print:
- 120 squares, 3⅜" x 3⅜"
- 174 squares, 2⅝" x 2⅝"

*Cut first.

Piecing the Blocks

1. On the wrong side of a white 3⅜" square, draw two diagonal lines from corner to corner with the marking tool of your choice. Place the white square on an indigo 3⅜" square, right sides together. Sew a ¼" seam on each side of one line. Cut on the unsewn line first, and then on the remaining drawn line to cut the sewn square into quarters. Press open to make pieced triangles. Make 480.

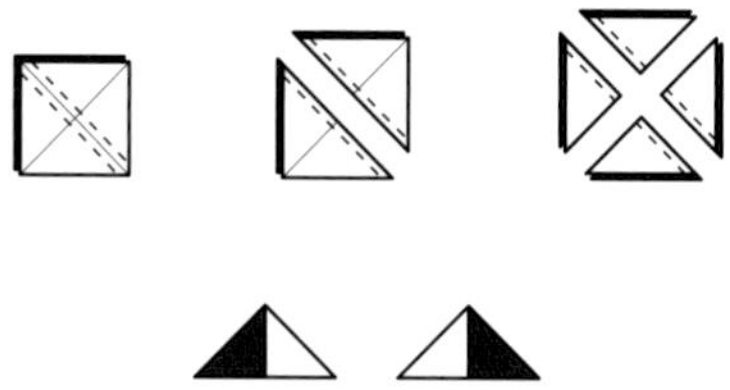

Make 480.

2. Stitch two pieced triangles together as shown to make a pieced square. Make 240.

Make 240.

3. Arrange and sew five rows using white 2⅝" squares, pieced squares, and indigo 2⅝" squares. Sew the rows together to complete an Ohio Star Variation block. Make 20.

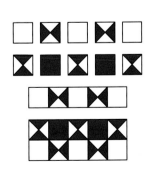 

Ohio Star Variation block.
Make 20.

4. For the side pieced border strips, arrange and sew together 25 indigo 2⅝" squares, white 4¼" quarter-square triangles, and white 2⅜" half-square triangles. Make two. In a similar manner, make top and bottom pieced border strips using 22 indigo 2⅝" squares, white 4¼" quarter-square triangles, and white 2⅜" half-square triangles. Make two.

Quilt-Top Assembly

Refer to the quilt assembly diagram at right for the following steps. The setting triangles on all edges and corners are cut oversized to allow trimming the quilt edges even before the pieced borders are added.

1. Arrange and sew eight diagonal rows using the blocks, the white 11⅛" squares, and the white 17" quarter-square triangles. Sew the rows together. Stitch the white 9" half-square triangles to the corners.

2. Measure the exact length and width of the center of the quilt, raw edge to raw edge. Measure the pieced border strips. Trim the top and bottom quilt edges even, making the length of the quilt the same as the length of the side pieced border strips. Trim the side quilt edges even, making the width of the quilt 6" narrower than the length of the top and bottom pieced border strips.

3. Stitch the side pieced border strips to the sides of the quilt. Sew the top and bottom pieced border strips to the top and bottom of the quilt. Sew white 9½" x 89" strips to the sides of the quilt; trim even with the top and bottom. Sew the remaining white strips to the top and bottom; trim even.

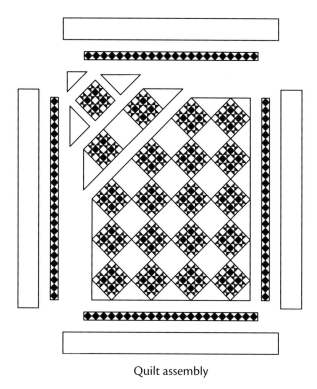

Quilt assembly

Quilting and Finishing

Layer, baste, and quilt (see "Finishing" on page 94). Kelly's lavish hand quilting is the real star of this quilt. She filled each alternate square and setting triangle with a feathered quatrefoil. The block patches and border strip pieces are ¼" outlined. The outer border features feathered vines with a background pattern of ¾" parallel lines. Bind the quilt with the white solid 2½" strips.

Snow Crystals

LIKE FROST ON A NIPPY MORNING,
LERLENE'S CRISP BLOCKS GLISTEN
AND GLOW. AND THE WARMTH
OF YOUR HOME WON'T MELT THE
FRESH APPEAL OF THIS TINSELED
TRIBUTE TO WINTER.

Designed by Lerlene Nevaril; machine quilted by Mary Roder of the Quiltworks, Merrill, Iowa

Finished quilt size: 71½" x 71½"

Number and size of finished blocks: 13 Snow Crystal blocks, 12" x 12"; 12 Snowflake blocks, 12" x 12"; 4 Border Corner blocks, 4" x 4"

Planning

Paying close attention to the color variations and reversing the orientation of some of the block units will assure successful construction of this intricate-looking, easy-to-sew pattern. To get the full frosty effect of Lerlene's design, plan to do some of your quilting with metallic thread, as Mary did here.

Fabric Requirements

Navy snowflake print (blocks), 1¼ yards

Pale blue mottled print (block background), 3⅝ yards

Bright blue snowflake print (blocks), 1¼ yards

Bright blue print (blocks), ¾ yard

Navy dot print (blocks, border, binding), 2 yards

Navy large print (border), 2 yards

Backing, 4½ yards

Batting, full-size

Cutting Instructions

Navy snowflake print:
   264 squares, 2" x 2"
   52 squares, 2⅜" x 2⅜"

Pale blue mottled print:
   156 rectangles, 2" x 3½"
   344 squares, 2" x 2"
   100 squares, 3½" x 3½"
   48 rectangles, 3½" x 5"
   16 squares, 1½" x 1½"
   16 rectangles, 1½" x 2½"

Bright blue snowflake print:
   104 squares, 2" x 2"
   52 squares, 2⅜" x 2⅜"
   96 rectangles, 2" x 3½"

Bright blue print:
   100 squares, 2" x 2"
   50 squares, 2⅜" x 2⅜"
   16 squares, 1½" x 1½"
   8 squares, 1⅞" x 1⅞"

Navy dot print:
   *4 strips, 2" x 64", pieced from 8 strips, 2" x 42"
   *8 strips, 2½" x 42" (binding)
   100 squares, 2" x 2"
   50 squares, 2⅜" x 2⅜"
   16 squares, 1½" x 1½"
   8 squares, 1⅞" x 1⅞"

Navy large print:
   4 strips, 4½" x 68", cut on the lengthwise grain

*Cut first.

Piecing the Blocks

1. On the wrong side of a navy snowflake print 2" square, draw a diagonal line with the marking tool of your choice. Place the navy square on a pale blue 2" x 3½" rectangle, right sides together and aligning raw edges. Stitch on the drawn line; trim away and discard the excess fabric. Press open. Repeat on the opposite end of the rectangle using a bright blue snowflake print 2" square to make a flying-geese unit. Make 52. Repeat the process to make 52 reversed flying-geese units as shown. In the same manner, use a pale blue 1½" x 2½" rectangle with bright blue print and navy dot 1½" squares to make a small flying-geese unit. Make 16.

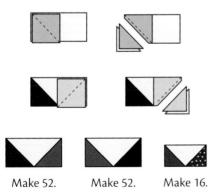

Make 52.　　　Make 52.　　　Make 16.

2. On the wrong side of a bright blue snowflake print 2⅜" square, draw a diagonal line. Place the bright blue square on a navy snowflake print 2⅜" square, right sides together. Sew a ¼" seam on each side of the marked line; cut apart on the marked line. Press open to make pieced squares. Make 104. In the same manner, use bright blue print and navy dot 2⅜" squares to make large pieced squares. Make 100. Repeat the process using bright blue print and navy dot 1⅞" squares. Make 16.

Make 104.　　Make 100.　　Make 16.

3. Arrange and sew together a navy snowflake print 2" square, two navy snowflake/bright blue pieced squares, and a pale blue 2" square to make a partial pinwheel unit. Make 52. In a similar manner, arrange and sew four large bright blue/navy dot pieced squares together to make a pinwheel unit. Make 25. Arrange and sew four small bright blue/navy dot pieced squares together to make a small pinwheel unit. Make four.

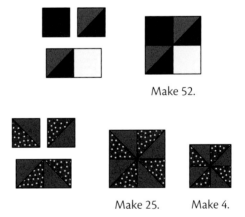

Make 52.

Make 25.　　　Make 4.

4. Watching the correct placement of fabrics, use the mark, stitch, trim, and press process from step 1 to add two navy snowflake print, one bright blue print, and one navy dot 2" square to the corners of a pale blue 3½" square to make a square-in-a-square unit. Make 52.

Make 52.

5. Using the mark, stitch, trim, and press process, add two pale blue 2" squares to opposite corners of a bright blue snowflake print 2" x 3½" rectangle to make a pieced rectangle unit. Make 48 of each arrangement shown, watching the direction of the stitching lines.

Make 48.   Make 48.

6. Arrange and sew together a pale blue 3½" square, two pieced rectangle units (opposite arrangements), and a pale blue 2" square as shown to make a corner unit. Make 48.

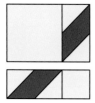 

Make 48.

7. Use the mark, stitch, trim, and press process to add bright blue print and navy dot 2" squares to a 3½" x 5" pale blue rectangle to make a block side unit. Make 48.

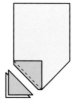  

Make 48.

8. Arrange and stitch five rows using four pale blue 2" squares, eight flying-geese units, four 2" x 3½" pale blue rectangles, four partial pinwheel units, four square-in-a-square units, and one pinwheel unit. Sew the rows together to make a Snow Crystal block. Make 13.

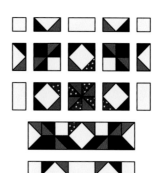 

Snow Crystal block.
Make 13.

9. To make a Snowflake block, arrange and stitch three rows using four corner units, four side units, and one pinwheel unit. Sew the rows together. Make 12.

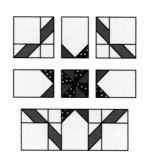 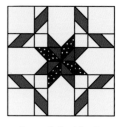

Snowflake block.
Make 12.

10. To make a Border Corner block, arrange and sew together four pale blue 1½" squares, four small flying-geese units, and one small pinwheel unit as shown. Make four.

Border Corner block.
Make 4.

Quilt-Top Assembly

Refer to the quilt assembly diagram for the following steps.

1. Arrange and sew five rows of five blocks each, alternating the blocks. Sew the rows together.

2. Measure the exact width of the quilt center from raw edge to raw edge. Trim two navy dot 2" x 64" strips to the exact width measurement; sew navy snowflake print 2" squares to both ends of the trimmed strips. Stitch the untrimmed 2" x 64" strips to the sides of the quilt; trim even with the top and bottom. Stitch the pieced strips to the top and bottom of the quilt.

3. Repeat the measure, trim, and sew process using the navy large print 4½" x 68" strips and the Border Corner blocks to make the outer borders.

Quilt assembly

Quilting and Finishing

Layer, baste, and quilt (see "Finishing" on page 94). Mary machine quilted a continuous swirl pattern in the block backgrounds. The navy dot border features a continuous loop, and Mary emphasized the design motifs in the large print border with quilting. Silver metallic thread was used to create a simple petal pattern in the center pinwheel section of each block, as well as holly leaf rosettes in the open spaces where the blocks join. Bind the quilt with the 2½" navy dot strips.

Road to Richmond

CIVIL WAR BUFF KELLY CORBRIDGE CHOSE A CLASSIC BLUE-AND-WHITE COLOR THEME AND A TRADITIONAL BLOCK TO HONOR A PERIOD OF TIME THAT TOUCHED EVERY AMERICAN. USE OUR SIMPLE TECHNIQUE TO MAKE THE HALF-SQUARE-TRIANGLE UNITS AND YOU'LL BE ENSURED A VICTORIOUS ENDING.

Designed by Kelly Corbridge; machine quilted by Julie Lambert

Finished quilt size: 63½" x 75½"

Number and size of finished blocks: 20 Road to Richmond blocks, 12" x 12"

Planning

Choose your favorite color and add white to make a picture-perfect quilt. Exact ¼" seam allowances are a must to ensure that these blocks go together easily.

Fabric Requirements

Assorted white prints (blocks), 1½–2 yards total

Assorted blue prints (blocks), 3–3½ yards total

White solid (blocks, border, binding), 4¼ yards

Backing (piece lengthwise), 4¾ yards

Batting, twin-size

Cutting Instructions

Assorted white prints—cut a total of:
 480 squares, 1⅞" x 1⅞"

Assorted blue prints—cut a total of:
 480 squares, 1⅞" x 1⅞"
 480 squares, 1⅞" x 1⅞"; cut in half diagonally to make 960 half-square triangles

White solid:
 *4 strips, 8" x 68", cut on the lengthwise grain
 *8 strips, 2½" x 42", cut on the crosswise grain (binding)
 160 squares, 3⅞" x 3⅞"; cut in half diagonally to make 320 half-square triangles

*Cut first.

Piecing the Blocks

1. On the wrong side of an assorted white 1⅞" square, draw a diagonal line from corner to corner with the marking tool of your choice. Place the white square on a blue 1⅞" square, right sides together. Sew a ¼" seam on each side of the marked line; cut apart on the marked line. Press open to make small pieced squares. Make 960 total.

Make 960.

2. Arrange and sew three small pieced squares and three blue 1⅞" half-square triangles together as shown to make a pieced triangle. Sew the pieced triangle to a white solid 3⅞" half-square triangle to make a large pieced square. Make 320 total.

Make 320.

Make 320.

3. Carefully arrange and sew four rows of four large pieced squares each as shown. Sew the rows together to make a Road to Richmond block. Make 20 total.

Road to Richmond block.
Make 20.

Quilt-Top Assembly

Refer to the quilt assembly diagram for the following steps.

1. Arrange and sew five rows of four blocks each. Sew the rows together.

2. Sew white solid 8" x 68" strips to the sides; trim even with the top and bottom. Stitch the remaining white strips to the top and bottom; trim even with the sides.

Quilting and Finishing

Layer, baste, and quilt (see "Finishing" on page 94). Julie machine quilted a curved outline in each blue triangle and added parallel lines (spaced ¼" apart) on the half-square triangles. A feather motif fills the white square created where four half-square triangles meet. A graceful feather floats on the border with crosshatching (lines spaced ½" apart) on the background. Bind the quilt with the 2½" white solid strips.

Quilt assembly

LONGING FOR SPRING?
CAPTURE BLUE SKIES, PUFFY
WHITE CLOUDS, AND RAYS OF
BRIGHT SUNSHINE WITH THIS
REFRESHING, EASY DESIGN.
CHOOSE BATIKS IN CHAMBRAY
BLUES TO PROVIDE JUST THE
RIGHT COLORS TO GET YOU
DREAMING OF THAT FIRST
WARM DAY.

Designed and quilted by Julie Sheckman

Fabric Requirements

White-on-white print (blocks), 1⅝ yards

Assorted medium blue-and-white batiks (blocks, outer border), 2–2¼ yards total

Assorted light blue-and-white batiks (blocks, outer border), 2¼–2½ yards total

Bright yellow mottled print (block centers, inner border), ⅝ yard

Blue batik (binding), ¾ yard

Paper-backed fusible web, ¼ yard

Backing (piece lengthwise), 5⅛ yards

Batting, twin-size

Cutting Instructions

White-on-white print:
    18 strips, 3" x 42"
Assorted medium blue-and-white batiks:
    17 sets of 4 matching strips, 1½" x 5½" (68 total)
    Cut a total of:
        9 strips, 3" x 42"
        10 strips, 5¼" x 10½"
        4 squares, 5¼" x 5¼"
Assorted light blue-and-white batiks:
    18 sets of 4 matching strips, 1½" x 5½" (72 total)
    Cut a total of:
        9 strips, 3" x 42"
        8 strips, 5¼" x 11½"
        6 strips, 5¼" x 10½"
Bright yellow mottled print:
    *2 strips, 1½" x 70½", pieced from 4 strips, 1½" x 42"
    *2 strips, 1½" x 52½", pieced from 3 strips, 1½" x 42"
    **35 squares, 1" x 1"
Blue batik:
    8 strips, 2½" x 42" (binding)

Cut first.
**Cut after preparing fabric with fusible web.*

Finished quilt size: 62" x 82"

Number and size of finished blocks: 35 blocks, 10" x 10"

Planning

Julie chose to use fused, raw-edge appliqué for her yellow squares. To speed the fusing process, the fabric is prepared with paper-backed fusible web prior to cutting the squares. If you wish to appliqué the squares using a turn-under seam allowance, you will have sufficient fabric to cut 35 squares, 1½" x 1½".

Julie used her binding fabric for some of the medium blue patches in the blocks. Do likewise if you wish. To ensure that the pieced border fits, use an accurate ¼" seam allowance throughout the construction.

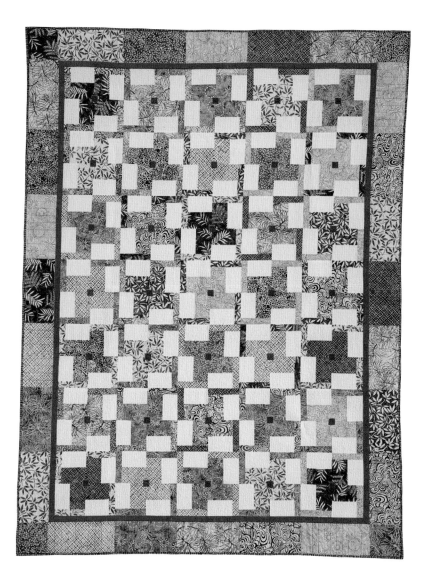

Piecing the Blocks

1. Sew a white and a medium blue 3" x 42" strip together. Make nine total. Press as shown. Cut 72 segments, 4½" wide. In the same manner, sew white and light blue 3" strips together. Make nine total. Press. Cut 68 segments, 4½" wide.

2. Watching the orientation, stitch a light blue 1½" x 5½" strip to the side of a white/medium blue segment to make a pieced square. Make 18 sets of four matching. In the same manner, sew a medium blue 1½" strip to the side of a white/light blue segment to make a pieced square. Make 17 sets of four matching.

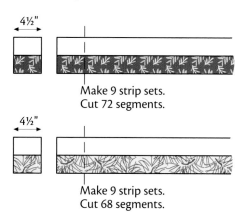

4½"

Make 9 strip sets.
Cut 72 segments.

4½"

Make 9 strip sets.
Cut 68 segments.

Make 18
sets of 4
matching.

Make 17
sets of 4
matching.

3. Stitch four matching pieced squares together. Following the manufacturer's instructions, fuse a prepared yellow 1" square to the center to complete the block. Make in the quantities and arrangements shown.

Make 18.   Make 17.

Quilt-Top Assembly

Refer to the quilt assembly diagram below for the following steps.

1. Stitch seven rows of five blocks each, alternating the blocks. Stitch the rows together.

2. Sew the yellow 70½" strips to the sides of the quilt. Stitch the yellow 52½" strips to the top and bottom of the quilt.

3. Alternating colors and watching placement, stitch two light blue 11½" strips, three medium blue 10½" strips, and two light blue 10½" strips together to make a side border. Make two and stitch them to the sides. In the same manner, stitch two medium blue 5¼" squares, two light blue 11½" strips, two medium blue 10½" strips, and one light blue 10½" strip together to make a top or bottom border. Make two and stitch to the top and bottom.

Quilting and Finishing

Layer, baste, and quilt (see "Finishing" on page 94). Julie used matching thread to machine quilt a meander on the blocks. Yellow thread was used to stitch squares in the yellow border and squares. The outer border was quilted with parallel lines 1" apart. Bind with the blue batik strips.

Quilt assembly

Blue Moon

SOMETHING RARE AND ENCHANT-ING, A BLUE MOON IS A SECOND FULL MOON IN ANY CALENDAR MONTH. CHARLOTTE ANGOTTI'S DESIGN IS ALSO A RARE THING: A TWO-BLOCK QUILT WITH AN ELEGANT, COMPLEX LOOK.

Designed and quilted by Charlotte Angotti

Fabric Requirements

Blue print (small star points), 1 yard

Assorted beige, cream, and tan prints (blocks, pieced border), 4⅛–4½ yards total

Beige floral (piecing, middle border), 1½ yards

Tan-and-blue print (block centers), ¼ yard

Cream-blue-and-green paisley (large star points), 1⅛ yards

Navy print #1 (piecing, outer border), 2 yards

Navy print #2 (blocks, pieced border), ¾ yard

Navy plaid (blocks, pieced border), ⅝ yard

Beige small plaid (binding), 1⅛ yards*

Backing, 8½ yards

Batting, king-size

*See "Planning" at left.

Finished quilt size: 91½" x 91½"

Number and size of finished blocks: 5 Star blocks, 16" x 16"; 4 Cross blocks, 16" x 16"

Planning

Creams, tans, and blues combine in this scrappy star quilt, perfect for using up some of your stash. We call for specific fabrics for most of the quilt, but feel free to use assorted same-color fabrics to make a quilt uniquely yours. Charlotte cut many of her beige patches from the binding fabric. You will have enough fabric to do likewise if you wish; just cut the binding strips first.

When making plastic templates (see "Making Templates" on page 89), include match points and grain lines. Make a small hole in the template plastic at each match point (use a large needle or stiletto). Place the template right side down on the wrong side of the fabric, trace around, and cut out the patch on the marked lines. For the A reversed pieces, flip the template so the wrong side is down on the wrong side of the fabric. Transfer the match points to the wrong sides of all A, A reversed, and B patches and align the match points when sewing. Watch orientation and positioning carefully throughout.

Cutting Instructions

Cutting instructions for templates are given on page 61.

Assorted beige, cream, and tan prints—cut a total of:
    79 squares, 3¼" x 3¼"
    23 squares, 9¼" x 9¼"; cut into quarters diagonally to make 92 quarter-square triangles
    74 squares, 2⅞" x 2⅞"; cut in half diagonally to make 148 half-square triangles
    57 squares, 2½" x 2½"
    14 rectangles, 4½" x 8½"
    4 squares, 4½" x 4½"

Beige floral:
    *4 strips, 2" x 88", pieced from 9 strips, 2" x 42"
    21 squares, 3¼" x 3¼"
    2 squares, 9¼" x 9¼"; cut into quarters diagonally to make 8 quarter-square triangles
    22 squares, 2⅞" x 2⅞"; cut in half diagonally to make 44 half-square triangles
    7 squares, 2½" x 2½"
    2 rectangles, 4½" x 8½"

*Cut first.

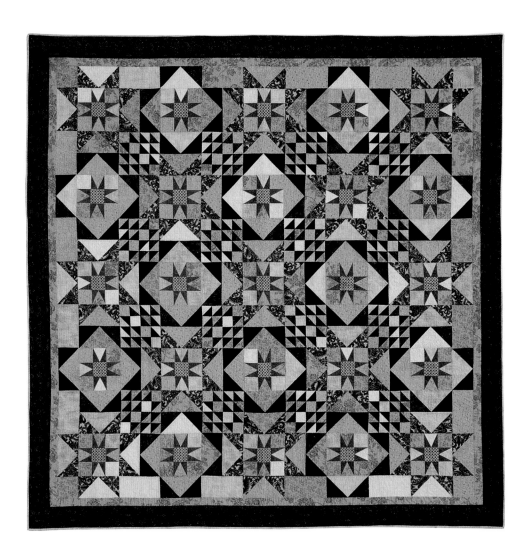

Tan-and-blue print:

25 squares, 3" x 3"

Cream-blue-and-green paisley:

52 squares, 4⅞" x 4⅞"; cut in half diagonally to make 104 half-square triangles

Navy print #1:

*4 strips, 4½" x 96", pieced from 10 strips, 4½" x 42"

16 squares, 4⅞" x 4⅞"; cut in half diagonally to make 32 half-square triangles

36 squares, 2⅞" x 2⅞"; cut in half diagonally to make 72 half-square triangles

Navy print #2:

16 squares, 4⅞" x 4⅞"; cut in half diagonally to make 32 half-square triangles

36 squares, 2⅞" x 2⅞"; cut in half diagonally to make 72 half-square triangles

Navy plaid:

16 squares, 4⅞" x 4⅞"; cut in half diagonally to make 32 half-square triangles

24 squares, 2⅞" x 2⅞"; cut in half diagonally to make 48 half-square triangles

Beige small plaid:

*10 strips, 2½" x 42" (binding)

Add remaining fabric to the assorted beige, cream, and tan prints.

Cut first.

Piecing the Blocks and Units

1. Sew a blue A and a blue Ar piece to the sides of an assorted beige B piece to make a star-point unit. Make 100 total. Sew three rows using four assorted beige or beige floral 3¼" squares, four star-point units, and one tan-and-blue 3" square. Sew the rows together to make a small star. Make 25 total.

Make 100.

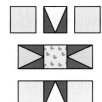

Make 25.

2. Stitch cream-blue-and-green paisley 4⅞" half-square triangles to the sides of a beige or beige floral 9¼" quarter-square triangle to make a pieced rectangle. Make 52 total. In the same manner, sew assorted navy 4⅞" half-square triangles to a beige or beige floral 9¼" quarter-square triangle to make a pieced rectangle. Make 48 total.

Make 52.   Make 48.

3. Sew together one assorted beige or beige floral and one assorted navy 2⅞" half-square triangle to make a pieced square. Make 192 total.

Make 192.

4. Sew two rows using two assorted beige or beige floral 2½" squares and two pieced squares. Stitch the rows together to make a star corner. Make 32 total.

Make 32.

5. Stitch together four pieced squares to make a cross corner. Make 32 total.

Make 32.

6. Sew three rows using four star corners, four paisley/beige pieced rectangles, and one small star. Stitch the rows together to make a Star block. Make five total.

 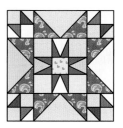

Star block.
Make 5.

7. In a similar manner, use four cross corners, four navy/beige pieced rectangles, and one small star to make a Cross block. Make four total.

Cross block.
Make 4.

8. Make a corner unit by stitching together one small star, two paisley/beige pieced rectangles, and one star corner. Make four total.

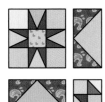

Corner unit.
Make 4.

9. To make a cross edge unit, stitch together three navy/beige pieced rectangles, one small star, and two cross corners. Make eight total.

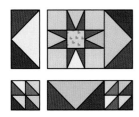
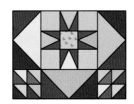

Cross edge unit.
Make 8.

10. In a similar manner, stitch together three paisley/beige pieced rectangles, one small star, and two star corners to make a star edge unit. Make four total.

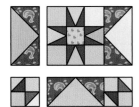

Star edge unit.
Make 4.

Quilt-Top Assembly

Refer to the quilt assembly diagram on the facing page and the photo on page 58 for the following steps.

1. To make the top and bottom rows, stitch together two corner units, two cross edge units, and one star edge unit each. To make the second and fourth rows, sew together two cross edge units, two Star blocks, and one Cross block each. To make the middle row, stitch together two star edge units, two Cross blocks, and one Star block. Arrange the rows in order and stitch the rows together.

2. For a pieced border strip, sew together three paisley/beige pieced rectangles, four assorted beige or beige floral 4½" x 8½" rectangles, and two navy/beige pieced rectangles. Make four. Sew a strip to each side of the quilt center. Stitch assorted beige 4½" squares to the ends of the remaining border strips. Stitch to the top and bottom.

3. Sew two beige floral 88" strips to the sides; trim even with the top and bottom. Stitch the remaining beige floral strips to the top and bottom; trim even with the sides. Stitch navy print #1 strips to the sides; trim even. Stitch the remaining navy print #1 strips to the top and bottom; trim even.

Quilting and Finishing

Layer, baste, and quilt (see "Finishing" on page 94). Charlotte machine quilted a leafy meander in the assorted beige patches and in the outer border. Bind with the beige small plaid strips.

TIP: Easy Cutting with Templates

Cut a strip of fabric that's 3¼" wide. Place the template on the fabric with the top and bottom edges of the template matching the long sides of the fabric strip. Cut along the two sides of the template. To cut both a regular and reversed template at the same time, place two strips of 3¼"-wide fabric right sides together with the edges matching. Place the template on the top fabric and cut both strips at the same time.

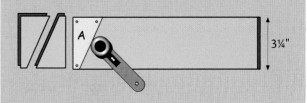

Quilt assembly

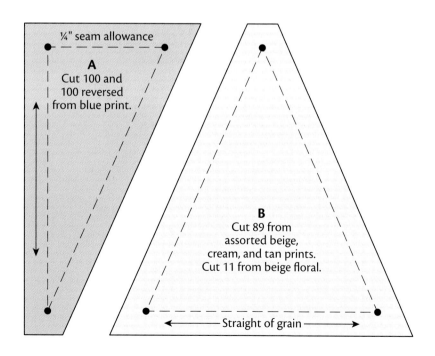

¼" seam allowance

A
Cut 100 and
100 reversed
from blue print.

B
Cut 89 from
assorted beige,
cream, and tan prints.
Cut 11 from beige floral.

← Straight of grain →

Red-White-
and-Blue Quilts

WHEN USED TOGETHER, THESE COLORS OFTEN EVOKE A PATRIOTIC

FEEL, BUT DON'T LIMIT THESE QUILTS TO BEING DISPLAYED ONLY

ON NATIONAL HOLIDAYS. THIS CHEERFUL COMBINATION WILL

LIFT YOUR SPIRITS ANY TIME OF THE YEAR.

Americana

NEED A STUNNING QUILT FOR
A MILITARY MEMBER, OR TO
SHOW YOUR PATRIOTIC PRIDE?
THIS ALL-AMERICAN DESIGN,
MADE WITH WOVEN COTTONS
AND FELTED WOOLS, IS A REAL
YANKEE-DOODLE DANDY!

Designed by Gerri Robinson;
machine quilted by Rebecca Segura

Finished quilt size: 62½" x 62½"

Number and size of finished blocks: 4 Americana
blocks, 16" x 16"

Planning

Gerri used an assortment of wools for the appliquéd stars and circles. If you choose to felt your own wool, be sure to purchase pieces larger than the felted sizes to allow for shrinkage during the felting process. To felt wool, wash and dry on high heat settings, cleaning the machine's lint trap often. The appliqué was added using paper-backed fusible web and the edges were secured with machine quilting. If you choose to do likewise, be sure to flop the templates before tracing them on the paper-backed fusible web. The appliqué patterns are printed without seam allowances.

Accurately sewing the ¼" seam allowances is a must to make the quilt center and borders fit together perfectly.

Fabric Requirements

Assorted dark blue prints (blocks, inner border, outer border), 1¼–1½ yards total

Assorted tan and white prints (blocks, outer border), 1⅝–2 yards total

Assorted tan or white tone-on-tone prints (sashing, inner border), 1¼–1⅝ yards total

Assorted red prints (blocks, outer border, pieced binding), 1⅝–2 yards total

Assorted medium blue prints (blocks, middle border), ⅞–1¼ yards total

4 red-and-black plaid felted wools (large corner stars), 8" x 8" piece each

Red-and-white plaid felted wool (small corner stars), 9" x 9" piece

Red felted wool (circles), 9" x 14" piece

Dark blue felted wool (small stars), 20" x 27" piece

Backing, 4 yards

Batting, twin-size

Paper-backed fusible web (optional)*

*See "Planning" at left.

Cutting Instructions

Cutting instructions for templates are given on page 69.

Assorted dark blue prints:

1 matching set of:
    5 squares, 2½" x 2½"
    4 squares, 6½" x 6½"
1 set of 2 matching strips, 4½" x 42"
2 sets of 2 matching strips, 2½" x 42"
Cut a total of:
    12 squares, 4⅞" x 4⅞"; cut in half diagonally to make 24 half-square triangles

Assorted tan and white prints:

2 sets of 2 matching strips, 2½" x 42"
1 set of 2 matching strips, 4½" x 42"
Cut a total of:
    8 squares, 4⅞" x 4⅞"; cut in half diagonally to make 16 half-square triangles
    48 rectangles, 2½" x 4½"
    80 squares, 2½" x 2½"

Assorted tan or white tone-on-tone prints—cut a total of:

　　4 squares, 4⅞" x 4⅞"; cut in half diagonally to make
　　　　8 half-square triangles
　　28 rectangles, 2½" x 4½"
　　20 squares, 6½" x 6½"

Assorted red prints:

　　4 sets of 2 matching strips, 2½" x 42"
　　Cut a total of:
　　　　32 squares, 2½" x 2½"
　　　　32 rectangles, 2½" x 4½"
　　　　7 strips, 2½" x 42" (binding)

Assorted medium blue prints:

　　4 matching sets of:
　　　　8 squares, 2½" x 2½"
　　　　1 square, 4½" x 4½"
　　Cut a total of:
　　　　20 strips, 2½" x 6½"
　　　　4 strips, 2½" x 10½"
　　　　4 strips, 2½" x 8½"

Piecing the Blocks

1. Sew dark blue and tan print 4⅞" half-square triangles together to make a pieced square; make 16 total. Repeat the process using dark blue and tan tone-on-tone 4⅞" half-square triangles; make eight and set aside for step 1 of "Piecing the Border Units" at right.

Make 16.   Make 8.

2. Draw a diagonal line on the wrong side of a red 2½" square. Place the red square on a tan print 2½" x 4½" rectangle, right sides together and aligning raw edges. Sew on the drawn line. Trim and discard the excess fabric; press open. Make 16 total. Repeat the process, rotating the marked square to the other side of the strip. Make 16.

Make 16.   Make 16.

3. Repeat the mark, stitch, trim, and press process using tan print 2½" squares on both ends of a red 2½" x 4½" rectangle to make a flying-geese unit. Make 32 total. Sew two pieced rectangles and two flying-geese units together to make a pieced strip. Make 16 total.

Make 32.

Make 16.

4. To make a center star, repeat the mark, stitch, trim, and press process using matching medium blue 2½" squares and tan print 2½" x 4½" rectangles to make four sets of four flying-geese units. Sew three rows using tan print 2½" squares, a set of four flying-geese units, and a matching medium blue 4½" square. Sew the rows together. Make four total.

Make 4 sets of 4.   Make 4.

5. Combine four pieced squares, four pieced strips, and one star from step 4 to make an Americana block. Make four total.

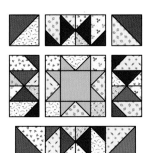 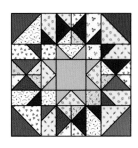

Make 4.

Piecing the Border Units

1. To make an inner-border unit, sew tan tone-on-tone rectangles to both sides of a dark blue 2½" square. Stitch the pieced squares from step 1 of "Piecing the Blocks" at left to a tan tone-on-tone rectangle. Sew the pieced strips together. Make four total.

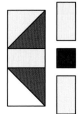 

Make 4.

2. To make the outer-border units, sew tan tone-on-tone, dark blue, and red strips together as shown. Make two of each. Press the seam allowances and cut 2½"-wide segments in the quantities shown. Sew four segments together for each unit. Make 24. The remaining segments will be used to complete the outer border in step 4 of "Quilt-Top Assembly" at right.

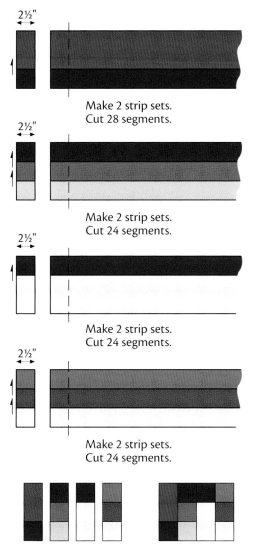

2½"

Make 2 strip sets.
Cut 28 segments.

2½"

Make 2 strip sets.
Cut 24 segments.

2½"

Make 2 strip sets.
Cut 24 segments.

2½"

Make 2 strip sets.
Cut 24 segments.

Make 24.

Quilt-Top Assembly

Refer to the quilt assembly diagram on page 68 for the following steps.

1. Sew four sashing strips using four tan tone-on-tone 2½" x 4½" rectangles each. Sew two block rows using two blocks and one pieced sashing strip each. Stitch two pieced sashing strips to the remaining dark blue 2½" square to make the center sashing strip. Stitch the block rows to the center sashing strip.

2. Sew two strips using four tan tone-on-tone 6½" squares and one inner-border unit each. Stitch to the sides of the quilt. Sew two strips of six tan tone-on-tone 6½" squares and one inner-border unit each; stitch to the top and bottom.

3. For the middle pieced border, sew two strips using six medium blue 6½" and one 10½" strip each; sew to the sides. Stitch two strips using two medium blue 8½" strips, four 6½" strips, and one 10½" strip each. Sew to the top and bottom.

4. Sew four strips of six outer-border units each. Sew one remaining blue/red 2½" segment (cut in step 2 of "Piecing the Border Units") to the end of each strip. Stitch a border to each side. Sew the dark blue 6½" squares to both ends of the remaining strips. Sew to the top and bottom.

5. Referring to the photo on page 65, position and appliqué wool shapes A–C using a machine or hand buttonhole stitch; or, secure with quilting, as in Gerri's quilt.

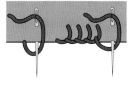

Buttonhole stitch

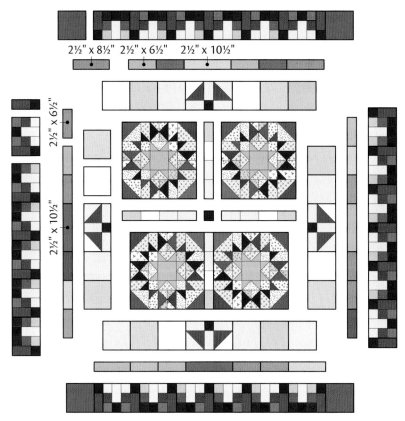

2½" x 8½"   2½" x 6½"   2½" x 10½"

2½" x 6½"

2½" x 10½"

Quilt assembly

Quilting and Finishing

Layer, baste, and quilt (see "Finishing" on page 94).
Rebecca machine quilted a spiral on each block. A
different meander fills the background of the quilt
center and each border. The appliqué pieces are outline
stitched.

To make the pieced binding, sew together the
assorted red 2½" x 42" strips in random order. Bind the
quilt with the pieced strip.

Trim and
press open.

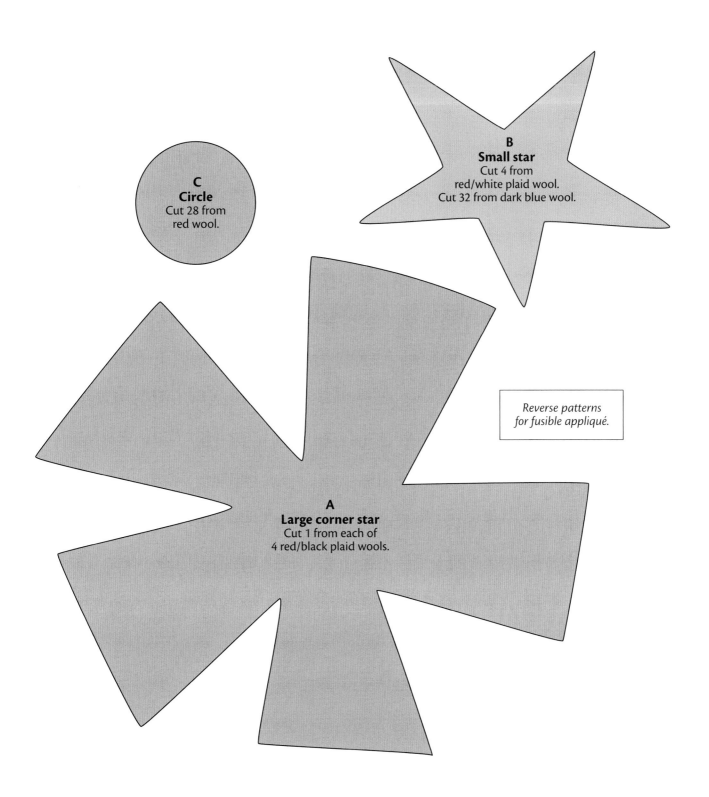

C
Circle
Cut 28 from
red wool.

B
Small star
Cut 4 from
red/white plaid wool.
Cut 32 from dark blue wool.

*Reverse patterns
for fusible appliqué.*

A
Large corner star
Cut 1 from each of
4 red/black plaid wools.

Prairie Pinwheels

SUNSHINE AND SHADOW PLAY ACROSS THE PRAIRIE AS THE BREEZE SPINS THESE PATRIOTIC PINWHEELS. A SUMMER CLASSIC, THIS SCRAPPY QUILT FEATURES FABRICS PIECED TOGETHER IN MATCHING SETS TO CREATE LARGE PATCHES OF SHIFTING SHADES.

Designed by Dolores Smith and Sarah Maxwell; machine quilted by Connie Gresham

Finished quilt size: 85½" x 109½"

Number and size of finished blocks: 48 Prairie Pinwheel blocks, 12" x 12"

Planning

Each of the 24 outer blocks in this intriguing quilt is made using one navy 4¼" square cut into quarter-square triangles and three matching 3⅞" squares; one matching set of tan patches; one set of matching medium blue patches; and one red 4¼" square cut into quarter-square triangles.

Each of the 24 inner blocks is made using two assorted red 4¼" squares cut into quarter-square triangles; one matching set of tan patches; one matching set of medium blue patches; and one set of three matching navy 3⅞" squares.

We recommend you group all the patches needed for each block before beginning construction. Dolores and Sarah cut a few of the matching sets of assorted tan prints from the cream-and-red small paisley used in the inner border to help unify the quilt. You will have sufficient fabric to do the same if you like. Just cut the border strips first, and then cut sets of matching patches as listed in the assorted tan print cutting instructions.

Fabric Requirements

Assorted navy prints (blocks), 2⅛–2⅜ yards total

Assorted tan and cream prints (blocks), 3⅞–4⅛ yards total

Assorted medium blue prints (blocks), 2⅜–2⅝ yards total

Assorted red prints (blocks), 1⅛–1⅜ yards total

Cream-and-red small paisley (inner border*), ¾ yard

Blue-and-red floral (outer border, binding), 3 yards

Backing (piece widthwise), 8 yards

Batting, king-size

*See "Planning" at left.

Cutting Instructions

Assorted navy prints:

    24 matching sets of:

        1 square, 4¼" x 4¼"; cut into quarters diagonally to make 4 quarter-square triangles (96 total)

        3 squares, 3⅞" x 3⅞" (72 total)

    24 sets of 3 matching squares, 3⅞" x 3⅞" (72 total)

Assorted tan and cream prints—cut 48 matching sets of:

    2 squares, 4¼" x 4¼"; cut into quarters diagonally to make 8 quarter-square triangles (384 total)

    3 squares, 3⅞" x 3⅞" (144 total)

    1 square, 4¾" x 4¾" (48 total)

Assorted medium blue prints—cut 48 sets of:

    4 matching squares, 3⅞" x 3⅞"; cut in half diagonally to make 8 half-square triangles (384 total)

Assorted red prints—cut a total of:

    72 squares, 4¼" x 4¼"; cut into quarters diagonally to make 288 quarter-square triangles

*Cream-and-red small paisley:

    2 strips, 2" x 100", pieced from 5 strips, 2" x 42"

    2 strips, 2" x 80", pieced from 4 strips, 2" x 42"

Blue-and-red floral:

    2 strips, 5½" x 104", cut on the lengthwise grain

    2 strips, 5½" x 90", cut on the lengthwise grain

    4 strips, 2½" x 104" (binding)

*See "Planning" at left.

Piecing the Blocks

1. Sew navy and tan 4¼" quarter-square triangles together to make a pieced triangle. Make four matching. Repeat to make four matching pieced triangles using red and tan quarter-square triangles.

Make 4.   Make 4.

2. Sew matching medium blue 3⅞" half-square triangles to the pieced triangles to make pieced squares. Make three navy and three red.

Make 3.   Make 3.

3. Draw a diagonal line on the wrong side of a tan 3⅞" square. Place the marked square on a navy square, right sides together. Sew a ¼" seam on each side of the marked line; cut apart on the marked line. Press open. Make six matching triangle squares.

Make 6.

4. Sew medium blue 3⅞" half-square triangles to opposite sides of a tan 4¾" square. Sew one navy and one red pieced triangle to the remaining sides to make a block center.

Make 1.

5. Sew a navy pieced square and a triangle square together. Sew to the side of the block center, watching orientation. Sew a red pieced square and a triangle square together; sew to the opposite side. Use the remaining pieced squares and triangle squares to sew the top and bottom block rows. Sew to the center row to make an outer Prairie Pinwheel block. Repeat steps 1 through 5 to make 24 blocks.

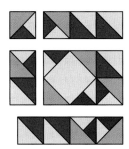 

Outer Prairie Pinwheel block.
Make 24.

6. In a similar manner, refer to the diagram to make inner Prairie Pinwheel blocks. Make 24 total.

Make 4.　Make 4.　Make 3.　Make 3.　Make 6.　Make 1.

 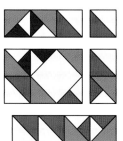

Inner Prairie Pinwheel block.
Make 24.

Quilt-Top Assembly

1. Stitch eight rows of six blocks each, watching the position and orientation. Sew the rows together.

2. Stitch the cream-and-red 100" strips to the sides; trim even with the top and bottom. Sew the remaining cream-and-red strips to the top and bottom; trim even with the sides.

3. Stitch the floral 104" strips to the sides; trim even. Sew the floral 90" strips to the top and bottom; trim even. See the quilt photo on the facing page.

Quilting and Finishing

Layer, baste, and quilt (see "Finishing" on page 94). Connie machine quilted paisley motifs on the block centers and on the squares formed where four blocks meet. The medium blue patches are filled with curved lines and each pinwheel is stitched with a spiral. The inner border is filled with a continuous leaf pattern and the outer border features more paisley motifs. Bind with the 2½" strips of blue-and-red floral.

Hometown Afternoon

RED, WHITE, AND BLUE FABRICS FROM YOUR STASH CREATE EASY PIECED BLOCKS FOR THIS PATRIOTIC BED-SIZED QUILT. ADD COORDINATING SASHING, BORDER, AND BINDING FABRICS, AND YOU'RE READY FOR AN ALL-AMERICAN NAP!

Finished quilt size: 75½" x 90⅝"

Number and size of finished blocks: 20 blocks, 12⅛" x 12⅛"

Planning

Quick and fun, this scrappy, sparkly quilt is a great stash buster. Have fun exploring your stash to come up with your favorite fabric combinations.

Fabric Requirements

White print (block backgrounds), 1⅜ yards

Assorted blue prints (blocks), 1⅝–2 yards total

Assorted red prints (blocks), 1⅛–1½ yards total

Light blue-and-white print (sashing posts), ½ yard

Red-and-white striped fabric (sashing), 1⅞ yards

Light blue-white-and-red print (border), 1¾ yards

Medium blue-and-white print (binding), 1 yard

Backing (piece widthwise), 7⅛ yards

Batting, queen-size

Designed by Sarah Maxwell and Dolores Smith; machine quilted by Connie Gresham

Cutting Instructions

White print:
40 squares, 5⅜" x 5⅜"; cut into quarters diagonally to make 160 quarter-square triangles
40 squares, 3" x 3"; cut in half diagonally to make 80 half-square triangles

Assorted blue prints—cut 40 sets of:
4 matching squares, 3⅜" x 3⅜" (160 total)

Assorted red prints—cut 20 sets of:
5 matching squares, 3⅜" x 3⅜" (100 total)

Light blue-and-white print:
30 squares, 3½" x 3½"

Red-and-white striped fabric:
49 strips, 3½" x 12⅝"

Light blue-white-and-red print:
4 strips, 6¼" x 84", pieced from 9 strips, 6¼" x 42"

Medium blue-and-white print:
10 strips, 2½" x 42" (binding)

Each block has only four fabrics.

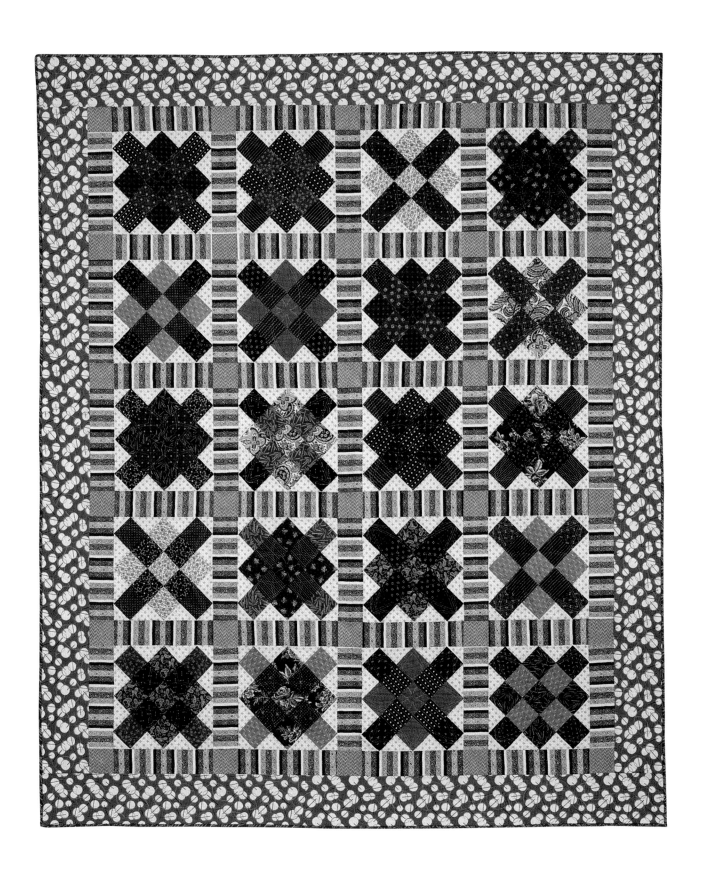

Piecing the Blocks

Each block contains two sets of blue 3⅜" squares and one set of red 3⅜" squares.

1. Stitch two white print 5⅜" quarter-square triangles to the sides of a blue 3⅜" square. Add a white 3" half-square triangle to make a pieced triangle. Make 20 sets of four matching.

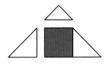 

Make 20 sets
of 4 matching.

2. Using five matching red and four matching blue 3⅜" squares, sew three rows as shown. Stitch the rows together to make a nine-patch unit. Make 20 total.

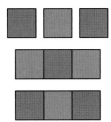 

Make 20.

3. Stitch four matching pieced triangles to the sides of the nine-patch unit to make a block. Trim the block to 12⅝" square if needed. Make 20 total.

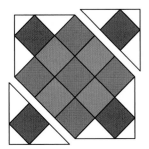 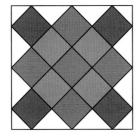

Make 20.

Quilt-Top Assembly

Refer to the quilt asssembly diagram and the photo on the facing page for the following steps.

1. Sew together five light blue-and-white 3½" squares and four red-and-white striped 12⅝" strips to make a sashing strip. Make six.

2. Stitch together five red-and-white striped strips and four blocks to make a block row. Make five total. Sew the sashing strips and block rows together, alternating them.

3. Sew light blue-white-and-red 84" strips to the sides; trim even with the top and bottom. Sew light blue-white-and-red strips to the top and bottom; trim even with the sides.

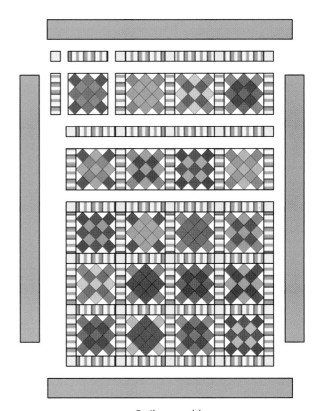

Quilt assembly

Quilting and Finishing

Layer, baste, and quilt (see "Finishing" on page 94). Connie machine quilted an eight-petaled motif in the blocks, quatrefoils in the sashing posts, and a stem-and-leaf design in the sashing. The border is filled with bat and baseball shapes. Bind with the 2½" strips of medium blue-and-white print.

Designed by Gerri Robinson; machine quilted by Rebecca Segura

Finished quilt size: 70½" x 70½"

Number and size of finished blocks: 8 A blocks, 12" x 12"; 8 B blocks, 12" x 12"

Planning

This unusual quilt features cotton prints, felted wools, and nine different striped cotton twills. Cut the striped rectangles and strips on the crosswise grain so that the stripes run in the direction shown in this quilt. Notice that the stars are the secondary pattern created when the blocks are sewn together. For this reason, it's important when assembling the blocks to be sure that the assorted red, medium blue, and dark blue patches are placed and oriented correctly. Careful piecing will ensure that the pieced borders fit well.

An assortment of red wools was used for the appliquéd stars. If you choose to felt your own wool, be sure to purchase pieces larger than the felted sizes to allow for shrinkage during the felting process. To felt wool, wash and dry on high heat settings, cleaning the machine's lint trap often. To cut the appliqué stars, refer to the template (page 83). The template is printed without seam allowances for use with paper-backed fusible web.

Fabric Requirements

Assorted red and blue striped fabric (piecing), 3–3½ yards total*

Assorted red prints (piecing, binding), 1⅜–1¾ yards total

Assorted medium blue prints (piecing), ⅝–⅞ yard total

Assorted dark blue prints (piecing), ⅝–⅞ yard total

Red-and-tan star print (border), ⅝ yard

Blue-and-tan star print (border), 1⅛ yards

Dark red felted wool (stars), 26" x 32" piece**

Paper-backed fusible web, 1½ yards

Backing, 4½ yards

Batting, full-size

Gerri used 100% cotton twill striped fabrics. The stripes run parallel to the selvage.

See "Planning" at left.

Cutting Instructions

Assorted red and blue striped fabric:
   Cut 16 matching sets of:
      1 square, 3⅞" x 3⅞"
      *2 strips, 3½" x 9½"
   Cut a total of:
      *64 strips, 3½" x 9½"
      *12 rectangles, 3½" x 6½"
      4 squares, 3½" x 3½"

Assorted red prints—cut a total of:
   **8 strips, 2½" x 42" (binding)
   4 squares, 3⅞" x 3⅞"
   52 squares, 3½" x 3½"

Assorted medium blue prints—cut a total of:
   8 squares, 3⅞" x 3⅞"
   32 squares, 3½" x 3½"

Assorted dark blue prints—cut a total of:
   4 squares, 3⅞" x 3⅞"
   40 squares, 3½" x 3½"

Red-and-tan star print:
   4 strips, 2" x 68", pieced from 8 strips, 2" x 42"

Blue-and-tan star print:
   4 strips, 4" x 74", pieced from 8 strips, 4" x 42"

Cut on the crosswise grain.

**Cut first.*

Piecing the Blocks

1. Position an assorted striped 3⅞" square right side up with the stripes running vertically. Draw a diagonal line on the wrong side of an assorted red 3⅞" square. Place the marked square on the striped square, right sides together. Sew a ¼" seam on each side of the marked line; cut apart on the marked line. Press open to make pieced squares. Using striped fabrics randomly, repeat to make units in the colors and quantities shown.

Make 4 pairs (red).

Make 4 pairs (medium blue).

Make 4 pairs (dark blue).

2. Watching the orientation, stitch a pieced square from step 1 to a matching striped 3½" x 9½" strip to make a half-square-triangle strip. Repeat to make strips in the colors and quantities shown.

Matching stripes

Make 8
(red triangles).

Make 16
(medium blue triangles).

Make 8
(dark blue triangles).

3. Draw a diagonal line on the wrong side of an assorted red 3½" square. Place the marked square on an assorted striped 3½" x 9½" strip, right sides together and aligning raw edges. Stitch on the drawn line; trim away and discard the excess fabric. Press open. Stitch an assorted red 3½" square to the end to make a pieced strip. Repeat to make strips in the arrangements, colors, and quantities shown.

Make 12 (red).

Make 16 (medium blue).   Make 12 (dark blue).

Make 4 (red).   Make 4 (dark blue).

TIP: Create a Design Wall

Use a design surface (felt-covered wall, large table, or other flat area) to place and check the units as you sew.

4. Stitch together one red and one medium blue strip from step 3 and one red and one medium blue half-square-triangle strip from step 2 to make block A. Make eight total. Stitch together one medium and one dark blue pieced strip and one medium and one dark blue half-square-triangle strip to make block B. Make eight total.

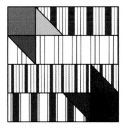 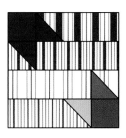

Block A.
Make 8.

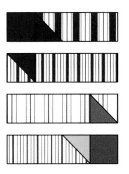

Block B.
Make 8.

5. Draw a diagonal line on the wrong side of an assorted red 3½" square. Place the marked square on a 3½" x 6½" striped rectangle, right sides together and aligning raw edges. Stitch on the drawn line. Trim and discard the excess fabric; press open. Repeat on the opposite end of the striped rectangle to make a pieced rectangle. Make eight total. Repeat using dark blue 3½" squares to make four dark blue units.

Make 8.   Make 4.

Quilt-Top Assembly

Refer to the quilt assembly diagram below and the photo on page 80 for the following steps.

1. Stitch four rows of four blocks each, watching the placement and orientation. Sew the rows together. Stitch together two red and two dark blue pieced strips to make a pieced border. Make four. Sew two to the sides of the quilt. Sew assorted red 3½" squares to both ends of the remaining pieced borders. Stitch to the top and bottom of the quilt.

2. Stitch together two red pieced rectangles, one blue pieced rectangle, and four striped 3½" x 9½" strips to make a pieced border. Make four. Stitch two to the sides of the quilt. Watching orientation, stitch striped 3½" squares to both ends of the remaining pieced borders. Sew to the top and bottom of the quilt.

3. Sew red-and-tan star print strips to the sides of the quilt; trim even with the top and bottom. Stitch the remaining red-and-tan star strips to the top and bottom; trim even with the sides. Repeat the process with blue-and-tan star print strips.

4. Use the pattern to trace star shapes on the paper side of paper-backed fusible web (see "Fusible Appliqué" on page 92). Cut apart, leaving a small margin beyond the drawn lines. Following the manufacturer's instructions, fuse to the wrong side of the dark red wool; cut apart on the drawn lines. Referring to the photo, fuse the stars in place following the manufacturer's instructions.

Quilt assembly

Quilting and Finishing

Layer, baste, and quilt (see "Finishing" on page 94). Rebecca machine quilted the background with an allover pebble design. Each pieced star is quilted in the ditch and the outer borders feature a continuous flower design. Rebecca appliquéd and quilted the wool stars at the same time by stitching a star and a swirl in each appliqué.

To make the pieced binding, sew the assorted red print 2½" x 42" strips together. Bind the quilt with the pieced strip.

Trim and press open.

Star
Cut 32 from assorted dark red wools.

Windswept

THIS QUILT SPINS AND DAZZLES
LIKE FIREWORKS! SEARCH YOUR
STASH FOR RED, CREAM, AND
BLUE PRINTS AND MAKE THIS
FABULOUS DESIGN FOR YOUR
FOURTH OF JULY PICNIC.

Designed and quilted by Ann Weber

Finished quilt size: 50½" x 50½"

Number and size of finished blocks: 100 Pinwheel blocks, 4" x 4"

Planning

Get ready to celebrate summer and our favorite red-white-and-blue national holiday. These lovely traditional Pinwheel blocks put the "spin" on summer fun. Use a wide variety of assorted blue prints to duplicate the feeling of movement in Ann's quilt.

Fabric Requirements

Assorted cream prints (blocks), 1½–1¾ yards total

Assorted dark blue prints (blocks), ⅞–1⅛ yards total

Assorted medium blue prints (blocks), ⅞–1⅛ yards total

Assorted red prints (sashing, binding), 1⅝–2 yards total

Assorted light blue prints (sashing posts), ¼–⅜ yard total

Backing, 3⅜ yards

Batting, twin-size

Cutting Instructions

Assorted cream prints—cut a total of:
    200 squares, 2⅞" x 2⅞"

Assorted dark blue prints—cut a total of:
    100 squares, 2⅞" x 2⅞"

Assorted medium blue prints—cut a total of:
    100 squares, 2⅞" x 2⅞"

Assorted red prints—cut a total of:
    *16 strips, 2½" x 20" (binding)
    200 squares, 2½" x 2½"

Assorted light blue prints—cut a total of:
    25 squares, 2½" x 2½"

*Cut first.

Piecing the Blocks and Sashing Strips

1. Draw a diagonal line on the wrong side of a cream 2⅞" square. Place the marked square on a dark blue 2⅞" square, right sides together. Sew ¼" from each side of the marked line; cut apart on the marked line. Press open to make pieced squares. Make 200. Repeat the process using cream and medium blue 2⅞" squares. Make 200.

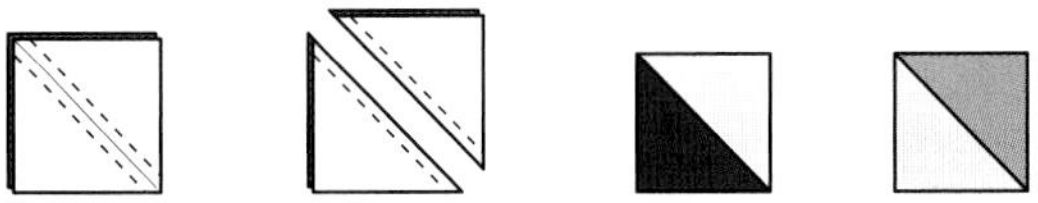

Make 200.   Make 200.

2. Sew four dark blue pieced squares together to make a Pinwheel block. Repeat with four medium blue pieced squares. Make 50 of each.

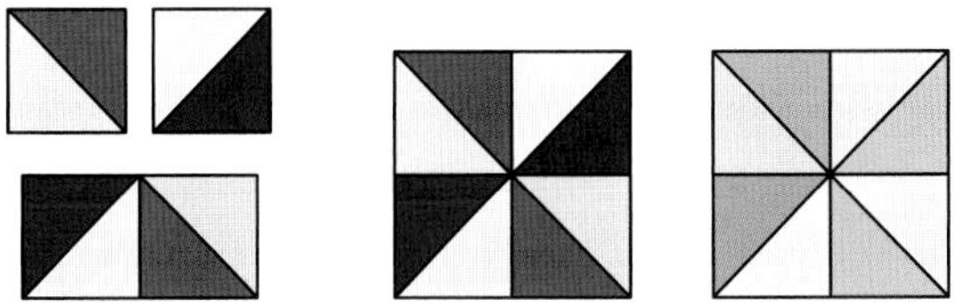

Pinwheel block.   Pinwheel block.
Make 50.   Make 50.

3. Sew one medium blue Pinwheel block and one dark blue Pinwheel block together to make a pieced rectangle. Make 16 total. Stitch two dark blue and two medium blue blocks together to make a pieced square. Make 16 total.

4. Sew two assorted red print 2½" squares together to make a short sashing strip. Make 20 total. Stitch four assorted red print squares together to make a long sashing strip. Make 40 total.

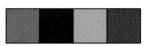

Short sashing.
Make 20.

Long sashing.
Make 40.

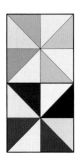

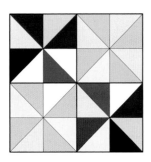

Pieced rectangle.
Make 16.

Pieced square.
Make 16.

Quilt-Top Assembly

Refer to the quilt assembly diagram below for the following steps.

1. Sew two Pinwheel blocks, five short sashing strips, and four pieced rectangles together, watching the color orientation. Make two for the top and bottom rows. Stitch five sashing rows using two short sashing strips, five assorted light blue squares, and four long sashing strips each. Sew four block rows using two pieced rectangles, five long sashing strips, and four pieced squares each.

2. Stitch the sashing rows and block rows together, alternating them as shown, to make the quilt center. Sew the top and bottom rows to the quilt center.

Quilting and Finishing

Layer, baste, and quilt (see "Finishing" on page 94). Ann machine quilted in the ditch along the seams. Diagonal crossed lines were stitched on the light blue squares. She added double wavy lines (approximately ¾" apart) centered on the sashing strips.

To make the pieced binding, sew the assorted red 2½" x 20" strips together in random order. Bind the quilt with the pieced strip.

Trim and press open.

Quilt assembly

Quiltmaking Basics

IF YOU ARE NEW TO QUILTING OR JUST NEED A REFRESHER, THE FOLLOWING TECHNIQUES WILL HELP YOU CREATE THE QUILTS IN THIS BOOK.

Rotary Cutting

For those unfamiliar with rotary cutting, a brief introduction is provided below.

1. To prepare the fabric, press to remove wrinkles. Fold the fabric and match selvages, aligning the crosswise and lengthwise grains as much as possible. Place the folded fabric on the cutting mat with the folded edge closest to you.

2. Align a square ruler along the folded edge of the fabric. Then place a long, straight ruler to the left of the square ruler, just covering the uneven raw edges of the left side of the fabric. Remove the square ruler and cut along the right edge of the long ruler, rolling the rotary cutter away from you. Discard this strip. (Reverse this procedure if you are left-handed.)

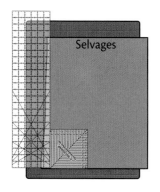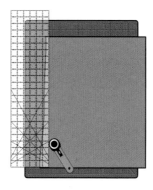

Selvages

3. To cut strips, align the required measurement on the ruler with the newly cut edge of the fabric. For example, to cut a 3"-wide strip, place the 3" ruler mark on the edge of the fabric.

4. To cut squares or rectangles, cut strips in the required widths. Trim away the selvage ends. Align the required measurement on the ruler with the left edge of the strip and cut a square or rectangle.

5. For half-square triangles, cut squares in half diagonally. For quarter-square triangles, cut squares into quarters diagonally.

Two half-square triangles cut from one square

Four quarter-square triangles cut from one square

Cutting Bias Strips

1. Position the fabric on the grid side of the cutting mat so that the lengthwise and crosswise grains of the fabric align with the vertical and horizontal grid lines.

2. Begin cutting approximately 6" from the lower-left corner of the fabric. Align the 45° line on the ruler with the first horizontal grid line visible on the mat below the fabric's bottom edge. Make a cut, creating a waste triangle.

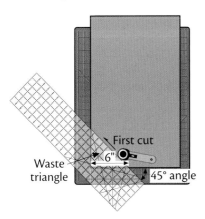

3. Align the required measurement on your ruler with the newly cut edge and cut the first strip.

4. Continue cutting until you have the number of strips required. Periodically recheck the position of the 45° angle marking on the ruler. If necessary, re-trim the cut edge of the fabric to true up the angle.

Making Templates

Templates may be used to mark and cut shapes that are not square or rectangular. Seam allowances are already included in patterns for piecing. The seam allowances are not added to patterns for appliqué.

1. To make permanent plastic templates, place template plastic over each pattern piece and trace with a fine-line permanent marker. Do not add seam allowances. Use a small ruler to draw straight lines on the templates.

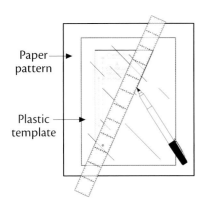

2. Cut out the templates directly on the drawn lines.

3. Use a permanent marker to write the pattern name and piece number (if applicable) on the right side of the templates. For piecing templates, mark the grain lines and place a dot where the seams cross.

4. Place the plastic template right side up on the right side of the fabric or place the template wrong side up on the wrong side of fabric and trace with a pencil or water-solvable marker. Either method will give you pieces with the same orientation as the pattern. To reverse the shape, flip the template so the wrong side is up on the right side of fabric or the right side is up on the wrong side of fabric.

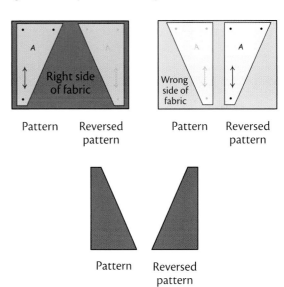

Machine Piecing

The most important thing to remember about machine piecing is to maintain a consistent ¼"-wide seam allowance. This is necessary for the seams to match and for the resulting block or quilt to measure the desired finished size. Measurements for all components of each quilt are based on blocks that finish accurately to the desired size plus ¼" on each edge for seam allowances.

Take the time to establish an exact ¼"-wide seam guide on your machine. Some machines have a special quilting foot that measures exactly ¼" from the center needle position to the edge of the foot. If your machine doesn't have such a foot, create a seam guide by placing the edge of a piece of tape or moleskin ¼" from the needle.

Appliqué

There are many techniques for appliqué and there's not space to cover all of them here. For additional information on other methods or more details, consult some of the many excellent books on the topic, or visit your local quilt shop to look into classes.

The first step for any method of appliqué except for fusible is to make a template either from plastic or from freezer paper. Plastic templates are more durable, and if one shape is repeated many times in the quilt, some quilters make a plastic template, which is then used to draw multiple freezer-paper templates. Freezer-paper templates will temporarily adhere to the fabric if the shiny side is placed face down on the fabric and pressed. You can reuse freezer-paper templates a few times before they will no longer stick to the fabric.

Basted-Edge Preparation

In this method, the edges of appliqué pieces are turned under and secured with a basting stitch before appliquéing by hand or machine.

1. Trace the appliqué pattern onto the dull side of freezer paper. Trace the pattern in reverse if it's asymmetrical and has not already been reversed for tracing. For symmetrical patterns, it doesn't matter.

2. Cut the freezer-paper template on the drawn lines and press it to the wrong side of the appliqué fabric.

3. Cut out the fabric shapes, adding a scant ¼" seam allowance around each shape.

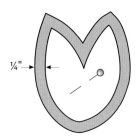

4. Turn the seam allowance over the edge of the paper and baste, close to the edge and through the paper. Clip the corners and baste the inner curves first. On outer curves, take small running stitches through the fabric only to ease in the fullness. Do not turn under edges that will be covered by another piece.

5. For sharp points, first fold the corner to the inside; then fold the remaining seam allowances over the paper.

Fold corners to inside.   Fold remaining seam allowances over paper.

6. When all seam allowances are turned and basted, press the appliqués.

7. Pin and stitch the pieces to the background by machine (see "Machine Appliqué" on page 91) or by hand with the traditional appliqué stitch (page 91).

8. After stitching, remove the basting stitches, carefully slit the background fabric behind the appliqué shape, and pull out the paper. Use tweezers if necessary to loosen the freezer paper.

Needle-Turn Hand Appliqué

With this technique, the edge of each piece is turned under with the edge of your needle as you stitch it to the background. Use a longer needle, such as a Sharp or Milliner's, to help you control the seam allowance and turn it under as you stitch.

1. Place the template right side up on the right side of the fabric and trace around it with a No. 2 pencil or a white pencil, depending on your fabric color and print.

2. Cut the shape out, adding a scant ¼" seam allowance all around.

3. Pin or baste the appliqué piece in position on the background fabric.

4. Beginning on a straight edge, bring your needle up through the background and the appliqué piece, just inside the drawn line. Use the tip of the needle to gently turn under the seam allowance, about ½" at a time. Hold the turned seam allowance firmly between the thumb and first finger of one hand as you stitch the appliqué to the background fabric with your other hand. Use the traditional hand appliqué stitch described at right.

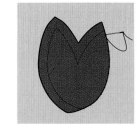

Traditional Hand-Appliqué Stitch

1. Thread a needle with a single strand of thread and knot one end. Use a thread color that matches the appliqué piece.

2. Slip the needle into the seam allowance from the wrong side of the appliqué, bringing it out on the fold line. Start the first stitch by inserting the needle into the background fabric right next to the folded edge of the appliqué where the thread exits the appliqué shape.

3. Let the needle travel under the background fabric, parallel to the edge of the appliqué; bring the needle up about ⅛" away through the edge of the appliqué, catching only one or two threads of the folded edge. Insert the needle into the background fabric right next to the folded edge. Let the needle travel under the background, and again, bring it up about ⅛" away, catching just the edge of the appliqué. Give the thread a slight tug and continue stitching.

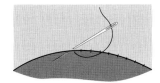

Appliqué stitch

4. Stitch around the appliqué, taking a couple of stitches beyond where you started. Knot the thread on the wrong side of the background fabric, behind the appliqué.

Bias Vines

Vines are narrow and curved, so it's best to cut them on the bias (page 88). The width to cut the strips will be given in the project instructions.

1. Fold the bias strips in half lengthwise, wrong sides together. Stitch ¼" from the raw edge and trim the seam allowance to ⅛".

2. Press the tube flat, centering the seam allowance on the back so the raw edge isn't visible in front. Using a bias bar makes pressing faster and easier.

Bias bar

Machine Appliqué

For the least visible stitches, use monofilament thread—clear for light-colored appliqués or smoke for medium or dark colors and a narrow zigzag stitch. If you want your stitches to show as a more decorative element, use a matching or contrasting-color thread in the top of your machine. Use a neutral-color thread to match your background fabric in the bobbin.

1. Set your machine for a small zigzag stitch (about ⅛" wide) and do a practice sample to test your stitches and tension. An open-toe presser foot is helpful for machine appliqué.

2. Prepare each appliqué piece using the basted-edge preparation method (page 90). Pin the pieces to the background and begin stitching with the pieces that are not overlapped by any other pieces.

3. Begin stitching with the needle just outside the appliqué piece and take two or three straight stitches in place to lock the thread. Make sure the needle is on the right of the appliqué and that the zigzag stitches will go into the appliqué piece. (You can use any decorative stitch on your machine.)

4. Stitch curved shapes slowly to maintain control, stopping and pivoting as needed.

Stop and pivot.   Continue stitching.

 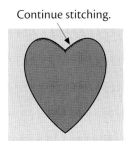

Stop and pivot.   Continue stitching.

5. Stitch completely around the appliqué until you are slightly beyond the starting point. Take two or three straight stitches in place to lock the thread and clip the thread tails.

6. To remove the freezer paper, carefully trim away the background fabric behind the appliqué, leaving a generous ¼" seam allowance to keep your appliqué secure. Use tweezers as needed. (Bias stems and vines and fused appliqué shapes will not have paper to remove, so it's not necessary to cut away the background.)

Fusible Appliqué

This appliqué method is fast and easy. Many fusing products are available, but fabrics do stiffen after application, so choose a lightweight fusible web. Follow the manufacturer's directions for the product you select.

Unless the patterns are symmetrical or the pattern has already been reversed, you must reverse the templates when you draw them on the paper side of the fusible web. Do not add seam allowances to the pieces, but leave a ¼" to ½" cutting margin around each shape drawn on the fusible web. For large appliqués, you can cut out the center of the fusible web, leaving a "donut" of web so that the centers of your appliqués will remain soft and unfused. Fuse the web to the wrong side of the appliqué fabric; then position and fuse to the quilt top.

For quilts that will be washed often, finish the edges of the appliqués by stitching around them with a decorative stitch, such as a blanket stitch (by hand or machine) or zigzag stitch.

Quilt-Top Assembly

Often blocks are sewn into rows, and then the rows are sewn together. Rows will sew together more easily if the blocks are pressed in the opposite direction from row to row.

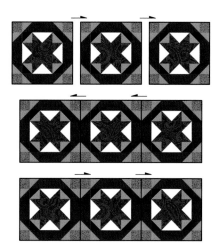

Sometimes sashing strips and corner squares are inserted between blocks and rows. Press in the direction of the sashing strips.

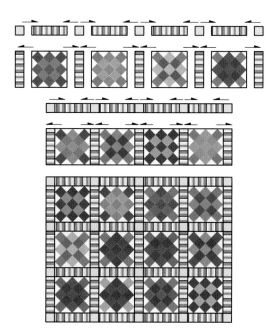

Blocks set on point need setting triangles on the sides and corners to make the quilt center square or rectangular. Often these triangles are cut oversized and then trimmed to square up the quilt center. When trimming oversized triangles, be certain to allow a ¼" seam allowance beyond the intersection of the setting triangles and the block points.

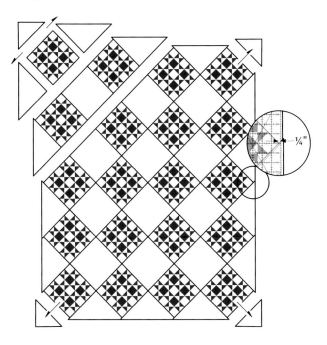

Borders

For best results, measure the quilt top before cutting and sewing the border strips to the quilt. Measure the quilt top through the center in both directions to determine how long to cut the border strips. This step ensures that the finished quilt will be as straight and as square as possible, without wavy edges.

Plain Borders

Many of these quilts call for plain border strips. Some of these strips are cut along the crosswise grain and joined where extra length is needed. Others are cut lengthwise and do not need to be pieced.

1. Measure the length of the quilt top through the center. Cut two borders to this measurement. Determine the midpoints of the border and quilt top by folding them in half and creasing or pinning the centers. Then pin the borders to opposite sides of the quilt top, matching the center marks and

ends and easing as necessary. Sew the border strips in place. Press the seam allowances toward the borders.

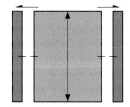

Measure center of quilt, top to bottom. Mark centers.

2. Measure the width of the quilt top through the center, including the side borders just added. Cut two borders to this measurement. Mark the centers of the quilt edges and the border strips. Pin the borders to the top and bottom edges of the quilt top, matching the center marks and ends and easing as necessary. Sew the border strips in place. Press the seam allowances toward the borders.

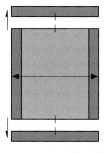

Measure center of quilt, side to side, including border strips. Mark centers.

Mitered Borders

1. Starting and stopping ¼" from the quilt corners and backstitching to secure, sew the border strips to the quilt top. Press the seam allowances toward the quilt center.

2. Fold the quilt on the diagonal at one corner, right sides together. Align the border-strip raw edges and border seams at the ¼" backstitched point; pin together.

3. Align a ruler edge with the fold, extending the ruler completely across the border. Draw a line from the backstitched point to the border raw edges. Stitch along the drawn line, backstitching at both ends. Press the seam allowances open. Trim the excess fabric to a ¼" seam allowance. Repeat for all corners.

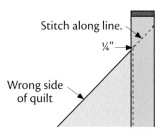

Stitch along line.

¼"

Wrong side of quilt

Finishing

The quilt "sandwich" consists of backing, batting, and the quilt top. Cut the quilt backing 4" to 6" longer and wider than the quilt top. Baste the layers together with thread for hand quilting or safety pins for machine quilting. Quilt by hand or machine.

Hand Quilting

To quilt by hand, you'll need short, sturdy needles (called Betweens), quilting thread, and a thimble to fit the middle finger of your sewing hand. Most quilters also use a frame or hoop to support their work.

1. Thread a needle with a single strand of quilting thread, knot one end, and insert the needle in the top layer about 1" from the place where you want to start stitching. Pull the needle out at the point where quilting will begin and gently pull the thread until the knot pops through the fabric and into the batting.

2. Take small, evenly spaced stitches through all three quilt layers. Rock the needle up and down through all layers until you have three or four stitches on the needle. Place your other hand under the quilt so that you can feel the needle point with the tip of your finger when a stitch is taken. Pull the thread through so it lies evenly on the fabric, being careful not to pull too tight.

3. To end a line of quilting, make a small knot close to the last stitch; then backstitch, running the thread a needle's length through the batting. Gently pull the thread until the knot pops into the batting; clip the thread at the quilt's surface.

Machine Quilting

For straight-line quilting, it's extremely helpful to have a walking foot to help feed the quilt layers through the machine without shifting or puckering. Some machines have a built-in walking foot; other machines require a separate attachment.

For curved designs or stippling, use a darning foot and lower the feed dogs for free-motion quilting. Free-motion quilting allows the fabric to move freely under the foot of the sewing machine. Because the feed dogs are lowered, the stitch length is determined by the speed at which you run the machine and feed the fabric under the foot. Practice on scraps until you get the feel of controlling the motion of the fabric with your hands.

Cutting Continuous Bias Strips from a Square

This technique provides a long strip of bias fabric without having to sew individual pieces together. Bias binding strips are stretchier than straight-grain binding and are used for curved and wavy quilt edges. Bias binding also rotates stripes and plaids so they run on the diagonal as in "*Célébrer!*" (page 33).

1. Remove the selvages from the fabric and cut a square as directed in the project instructions. (A 40" square should make about 16 yards of 2½"-wide bias strip.)

2. Lightly label the square as shown. Cut the square in half diagonally to make triangles.

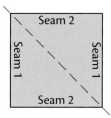

Seam 2

Seam 1

Seam 1

Seam 2

3. With right sides together and raw edges aligned, join the triangles (seam 1) to form a parallelogram. Press the seam allowances open. Measure and mark

across the parallelogram with lines equal to the width of your bias strip as shown.

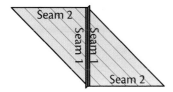

4. Form a tube by aligning the edges marked seam 2, matching your marked lines and offsetting the edge one strip width beyond the line. Stitch and press the seam allowances open.

5. Starting at the offset end, cut around the tube on the marked lines to make a continuous bias strip.

Binding

The quilt directions tell you how wide to cut the strips for binding. Bindings are generally cut anywhere from 2" to 2½" wide, depending on personal preference. You will need enough strips to go around the perimeter of the quilt plus 12". If you cut a continuous bias binding strip, begin the following instructions in step 2.

1. Sew the strips together end to end to make one long piece of binding. Join the strips at right angles and stitch from corner to corner. Trim the excess fabric and press the seam allowances open.

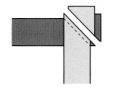

2. Trim one end of the binding strip at a 45° angle. Turn under ¼" and press.

3. Fold the strip in half lengthwise, wrong sides together, and press.

4. Trim the batting and backing even with the quilt top.

5. Starting in the middle of one side and using a ¼"-wide seam allowance, stitch the binding to the quilt. Keep the raw edges even with the quilt-top edge. Begin stitching 1" to 2" from the start of the binding. End the stitching ¼" from the corner of the quilt and backstitch. Clip the thread.

6. Turn the quilt so that you will be stitching along the next side. Fold the binding up, away from the quilt; then fold it back down onto itself, even with the raw edge of the quilt top.

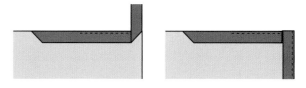

7. Stitch from the fold of the binding along the second edge of the quilt top, stopping ¼" from the corner as before. Repeat the stitching and mitering process on the remaining edges and corners.

8. When you reach the starting point, cut the end 1" longer than needed and tuck the end inside the beginning. Stitch the rest of the binding.

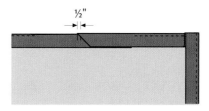

9. Fold the binding over the raw edges of the quilt to the back and blindstitch in place.

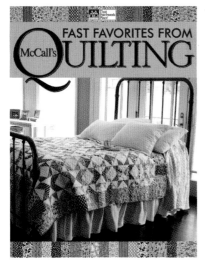
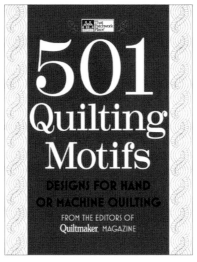
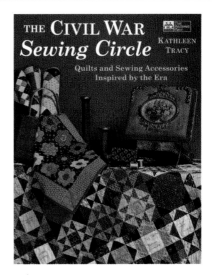
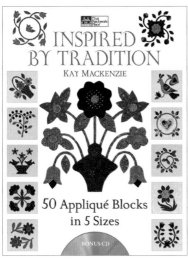

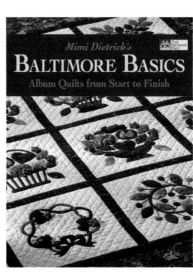